ARTIFICIAL INTELLIGENCE (AI) IN FAST FOOD CHAINS

CONCEPTS AND PRACTICAL ACTIONS

R. Brissi

Acknowledgment

To my dear wife Sara, my eternal partner and an inexhaustible source of inspiration. Your presence by my side not only strengthens me but also enriches everything I do. Every word in this book was shaped with your constant encouragement, brilliant insights, and meticulous reviews, making this project more complete and meaningful. I am deeply grateful for all the support, patience, and dedication you always show. Your participation was fundamental for this book to reach its true potential. I am immensely grateful that we shared yet another achievement together.

Summary

- Acknowledgment _____ 2
- Introduction _____ 4
- Chapter 1 | The Potential of AI in Fast Food Chains _____ 7
- Chapter 2 | Automation of Customer Service _____ 12
- Chapter 3 | Personalization and Smart Marketing _____ 17
- Chapter 4 | Inventory Management and Demand Forecasting _ 22
- Chapter 5 | Automated Logistics and Delivery Optimization ___ 28
- Chapter 6 | Team and Human Resources Management _____ 34
- Chapter 7 | Scalability with AI and Automated Systems _____ 40
- Chapter 8 | Omnichannel Integration: AI in Apps, Websites and Physical Locations _____ 46
- Chapter 9 | Efficient Communication Between Franchisors and Franchisees _____ 52
- Chapter 10 | Training and Retraining Franchisees _____ 59
- Chapter 11 | Franchisee and Franchise Unit Performance Evaluation _____ 65
- Chapter 12 | The Path to ESG Commitment _____ 71
- Chapter 13 | Continuous Evaluation and Monitoring _____ 78
- Chapter 14 | Challenges and Considerations _____ 84
- Chapter 15 | The Future of AI in Fast Food Chains _____ 91
- Author's Final Considerations _____ 94
- Glossary _____ 97

INTRODUCTION

The implementation of Artificial Intelligence (AI) in fast food franchises addresses a growing demand for solutions that enable scalability and the standardization of operations. With increasing competition in the franchise sector and high employee turnover, the need to adopt cutting-edge technologies to ensure the sustainability and growth of franchise networks becomes increasingly evident. Furthermore, both franchisors and franchisees face significant challenges in hiring skilled and unskilled workers. According to the 2024 Annual Franchisor Survey conducted by the International Franchise Association (IFA), 80% of franchisors reported difficulties in filling positions at their units, which further underscores the need for technological solutions like Artificial Intelligence (AI) to automate processes and reduce dependence on human labor.

Franchise networks face the challenge of maintaining brand consistency across all units, which is crucial for attracting new customers and franchisees. This includes the standardization of promotional materials, logos, images, and themes to ensure that the brand identity remains strong and recognizable in any market. Additionally, franchises must manage high operational costs, as national franchise brands often have higher initial fees, franchise costs, and royalties compared to regional brands.

Another constant challenge is adapting to industry changes. The business landscape is continuously evolving, and franchises need to be prepared to adjust to shifting consumer preferences, new regulations, and technological innovations. In this context, AI is not just a strategic tool but a necessity for networks seeking efficiency, flexibility, and competitiveness.

Building strong relationships between franchisors and franchisees is also crucial for long-term franchise success. Well-managed and robust relationships can determine a franchise network's ability to thrive and expand, while weak relationships can harm the overall operation. However, these relationships can be undermined by compliance issues, which, if unresolved, can lead to fines, litigation, and even more severe problems such as accidents or business disruptions.

Another important factor to consider is the level of digital competence among franchisees. In the digital age, franchisees have varying levels of technological proficiency, which can make the uniform implementation of more advanced systems, such as AI, challenging. To address this issue, it is essential to build a solid infrastructure with standardized systems and procedures, as well as continuous support, allowing even less tech-savvy franchisees to operate efficiently.

Additionally, effective communication is indispensable, both in customer relations and team management within the franchise. Franchisees need proper tools to communicate effectively with all stakeholders, and this is where AI can facilitate communication flows by automating processes and integrating systems.

Entrepreneurs and industry professionals are increasingly seeking practical content that shows how to apply AI in their businesses, not just conceptually but with concrete solutions that can be implemented. This book positions itself as a true consultancy, offering a comprehensive and practical approach to implementing AI in franchise networks. Each chapter is structured not only to explain the concepts but also to guide the reader through practical actions, detailing how each step of automation can be applied to their business.

Throughout the chapters, you will discover real-world examples and practical strategies that can be applied immediately, turning theory into action. Each page will provide valuable insights to revolutionize your approach and enhance the success of your franchise network. Get ready to explore the power of AI and take your business to a new level of efficiency and innovation!

CHAPTER 1 | THE POTENTIAL OF AI IN FAST FOOD CHAINS

Artificial Intelligence (AI) is rapidly transforming the fast food industry, one of the most competitive and dynamic markets in the global economy. Fast food chains, which traditionally rely on manual and repetitive processes to serve large volumes of customers, are embracing technology to optimize operations, enhance customer experience, and increase operational efficiency. The potential of AI in this sector is immense, encompassing everything from automating customer service to intelligent inventory management, marketing, and logistics.

One of the greatest advantages of AI for fast food chains is the ability to automate processes that previously required significant human involvement. Voice recognition systems, for instance, are increasingly being used in drive-thrus, allowing orders to be taken quickly and accurately. These systems are trained to understand language variations and background noise, offering efficient service even during peak hours. As a result, fast food chains can increase the number of customers served per hour, ensuring faster service and reducing lines, which is essential for success in this sector.

Automation also extends to self-service kiosks, which use virtual assistants and interactive interfaces to allow customers to place their orders independently. These AI-equipped kiosks can personalize the experience based on the customer's purchase history and previously recorded preferences. By collecting and processing this data, AI can suggest product combinations and promotions that increase the average ticket value, all in an automated manner. This not only improves the customer experience, making them feel valued and personally attended to, but also increases the operation's profitability.

Beyond customer service, AI also plays a crucial role in inventory management and demand forecasting. Historically, fast food chains have faced challenges related to inventory control, such as predicting demand fluctuations and managing perishable products. By using machine learning, AI algorithms can analyze historical sales data, seasonality, and even external variables like weather and local events to accurately forecast future demand. This allows chains to adjust their orders and stock levels more efficiently, preventing waste and ensuring that the right ingredients are always available at the right time.

The ability of AI to predict and adjust demand not only optimizes inventory but also generates significant savings for fast food chains. With more precise inventory management, it is possible to reduce food waste and minimize costs associated with storing excess products. This, in turn, enhances operational efficiency and allows chains to achieve healthier profit margins, maintaining long-term sustainability. AI, therefore, is not just an optimization tool but an essential component for the growth and scalability of fast food chains.

Another area where AI shows its full potential is in personalized marketing. By collecting and analyzing customer data, AI can identify patterns and preferences, allowing for precise audience segmentation. This enables fast food chains to create highly targeted marketing campaigns that directly address customers' interests and needs. For example, if a customer frequents a particular location at specific times, AI can send personalized promotions and notifications just before those times, increasing the likelihood of conversion and enhancing brand engagement.

Moreover, predictive analytics is a powerful tool for adjusting campaigns in real time. Based on variables such as weather, purchasing behavior, and local events, AI automatically adjusts offers and promotions, ensuring they are always aligned with current circumstances. This is particularly useful during holidays or sporting events when demand for certain products increases significantly. With AI, fast food chains can prepare in advance for these peaks, ensuring smooth operations and maximizing sales.

Logistics, in turn, is another crucial aspect for the success of fast food chains that greatly benefits from AI. The supply chain, which includes everything from sourcing fresh ingredients to delivering finished products, needs to be accurate and efficient for operations to be sustainable. AI can automate and optimize delivery routes, taking into account factors such as real-time traffic, weather conditions, and the proximity of units. With advanced algorithms, AI automatically adjusts these routes to ensure that products arrive on time and in the most efficient manner, reducing logistical costs and ensuring uninterrupted operations.

In addition to logistical efficiency, AI is also capable of identifying operational problems before they become critical. With real-time monitoring of operations, AI can detect anomalies in equipment performance or process efficiency, alerting managers so that interventions can be carried out quickly. For instance, if a refrigeration system is about to fail, AI can send a preventive alert so that maintenance is performed before the failure affects stock or disrupts operations. This proactive approach not only minimizes disruptions but also reduces maintenance costs by preventing more complex and costly issues.

The potential of AI in fast food chains is vast, impacting virtually every aspect of operations. From automating customer service and managing inventory to intelligent marketing and optimized logistics, AI enables these chains to operate more swiftly, efficiently, and profitably. The ability to personalize service, predict demand, and adjust operations in real time transforms how fast food chains function, creating a more flexible business model ready for the future. The adoption of these technologies is not just a competitive advantage; it is a necessity for those chains that want to expand and adapt to an ever-evolving market.

As we progress through this book, we will explore each of these areas in detail, offering insights into how AI can be implemented practically and effectively, maximizing its benefits and preparing fast food chains for a future of continuous growth and innovation.

Practical Action

To begin exploring the potential of AI in your fast food chain, the first step is to conduct a detailed mapping of current operations. Evaluate each stage of the process, from customer service to logistics, to identify areas that could be automated or optimized with AI. Consider aspects such as the frequency of repetitive tasks, execution time, and associated costs. From this analysis, identify which processes could benefit from intelligent automation, such as implementing smart chatbots that use Natural Language Processing (NLP) for customer service, demand forecasting systems for inventory control, or optimization algorithms for logistics. This initial mapping will serve as the foundation for implementing effective AI solutions in the following steps.

Currently, there are several chatbot tools on the market offering advanced features and easy integration with CRM and ERP systems. Chatbots like Ada, Drift, Intercom, ManyChat, and Chatfuel are examples suitable for fast food chains, each with its specific features. Configure these chatbots to provide automated and efficient initial customer service, ensuring a seamless transition to a human agent when the customer requires more detailed assistance.

Chapter 2 | Automation of Customer Service

Customer service is one of the most critical areas for the success of fast food chains. The speed, accuracy, and efficiency with which orders are processed can make a significant difference in the customer experience and, consequently, the franchise's performance. In this context, Artificial Intelligence (AI) emerges as a powerful solution to automate and optimize customer service, ensuring that fast food chains can handle growing volumes of customers efficiently and personally, regardless of the interaction channel.

With the increasing popularity of self-service kiosks and virtual assistants, fast food chains are redesigning their operations to incorporate cutting-edge technology. These kiosks, equipped with AI systems, allow customers to place their orders autonomously and quickly, without the need for direct interaction with staff. AI ensures that the interface is intuitive and personalized, recording the customer's previous preferences to suggest additional items or specific promotions, increasing the average ticket value and customer satisfaction. This approach makes the process faster and more efficient, especially during peak hours when queues tend to be longer.

Voice recognition technology also plays a crucial role, particularly in drive-thrus where speed is essential. Advanced AI systems are trained to interpret customers' verbal commands, even in environments with external noise or varying accents. These systems are designed to quickly understand and process orders with high accuracy, significantly reducing wait times. This eliminates the need for direct human interaction in many of these transactions, not only optimizing service time but also minimizing common errors caused by misunderstandings between attendants and customers.

Cameras positioned along drive-thru lanes can capture images of license plates. Using this data, AI can recommend items based on customers' previous orders, improving upselling and further reducing order time. With this integration, fast food chains can efficiently personalize suggestions, enhancing both the customer experience and operational performance.

The automation of customer service with AI is not limited to kiosks or drive-thrus. Fast food chains are also investing in virtual assistants and chatbots that operate on mobile apps and websites, providing a consistent, multichannel experience. These virtual assistants are programmed with Natural Language Processing (NLP), which allows them to interpret customer questions and requests accurately, as if they were conversing with a human agent. From answering frequently asked questions, such as opening hours and nutritional information, to facilitating orders and payments, these automated systems are designed to offer comprehensive and efficient support, available 24/7.

AI implementation in customer service also enables real-time personalization. By collecting data and continuously monitoring customer behavior, AI can adapt service and product suggestions for each individual. For example, if a customer frequently orders vegetarian products, the system can automatically suggest new options or combinations aligned with their preferences. Personalization significantly increases customer engagement and satisfaction while providing the fast food chain with an opportunity to boost sales through targeted offers and promotions.

Beyond personalization and speed, automating customer service offers substantial operational benefits. Reducing human involvement in repetitive tasks allows the chain's staff to be redirected to more complex and value-added activities, such as overseeing unit operations and interacting with customers who require more specialized assistance. This also reduces the need for continuous training of employees for these basic functions, which, in turn, lowers operational costs and increases overall efficiency.

Automating customer service with AI also ensures a high level of consistency. While human service can vary depending on an employee's skill, experience, or even mood, AI systems provide a standardized service, ensuring that every customer receives the same quality of care, regardless of the unit or channel used. This is crucial for maintaining brand reputation and ensuring that the customer experience is consistent across all interactions.

However, the adoption of automation in customer service requires careful planning. It is important that fast food chains choose AI platforms that are integrable with their existing systems, such as the point of sale (POS) and inventory management systems. Integration is essential to ensure that data flows continuously between systems, allowing AI to access updated information to personalize service and adjust recommendations in real time. Furthermore, it is critical to test these technologies in pilot units before expanding them to the entire network, ensuring that the systems work as expected and meet customer expectations.

Another crucial factor is ensuring customer acceptance and adoption of these new technologies. Even with the growing acceptance of self-service kiosks and virtual assistants, it is still essential for chains to educate their customers on how to use these tools efficiently. Introduction programs, promotional discounts for those using self-service, and intuitive interfaces are some of the strategies that can be employed to ease this transition.

In summary, automating customer service with AI is an irreversible trend and an opportunity for fast food chains looking to stand out in a competitive market. With technologies that improve order accuracy, reduce service time, and personalize the customer experience, AI enables these chains to operate more effectively and on a larger scale. When properly implemented, automation not only reduces costs and increases efficiency but also strengthens the relationship between the brand and consumers, ensuring that every interaction is an opportunity for customer loyalty and engagement.

PRACTICAL ACTION

To implement customer service automation with AI in your fast food chain, start by choosing a strategic entry point. Test the technology in a controlled environment, such as a pilot unit, using a voice recognition system in the drive-thru or a self-service kiosk. Closely monitor performance and customer acceptance, making adjustments as needed to ensure the system operates efficiently and intuitively. Gradually expand the technology to other units, always focusing on integration and personalization to maximize both operational and customer experience benefits.

As mentioned in the previous chapter, there are several chatbot tools currently available, such as Ada, Drift, Intercom, ManyChat, Chatfuel, Tars, and Freshchat, each offering specific features that can be tailored to the needs of fast food chains.

CHAPTER 3 |
PERSONALIZATION AND SMART MARKETING

In the highly competitive fast food sector, a brand's ability to connect directly with its customers and understand their preferences can be the decisive factor between success and failure. Artificial Intelligence (AI) is revolutionizing marketing, allowing fast food chains to personalize their campaigns and adjust their strategies in real-time, reaching audiences more precisely and efficiently. With AI, these chains are not merely collecting data on customer behavior; they are transforming this data into valuable insights that enable direct, segmented communication, creating more meaningful and impactful experiences for the consumer.

Over the past decades, digital marketing has become a powerful tool for brands seeking to increase their presence and influence. However, with the emergence of AI, marketing has shifted from a generic approach to a personalized strategy, where every customer interaction can be tailored based on purchase history, preferences, and even external variables such as weather or local events. This creates a scenario where marketing campaigns not only target a generic audience but speak directly to each customer in a unique way, enhancing the relevance and effectiveness of messages.

Personalization is one of the most powerful features of AI applied to marketing. By integrating machine learning systems that monitor customer behavior across apps, websites, and physical stores, fast food chains can create detailed profiles of each consumer. With these profiles, AI can suggest specific products and promotions based on individual preferences and purchase history. For example, if a customer frequently orders vegetarian meals or specific items at certain times, the system can send personalized offers and promotions shortly before those times, encouraging purchases and increasing loyalty.

Moreover, AI allows fast food chains to adapt their campaigns in real-time. AI-powered predictive analytics can anticipate how specific factors, such as weather or sporting events, may impact sales. For instance, on cold days, AI can automatically adjust campaigns to promote hot beverages or comfort foods, while on warmer days, the focus may shift to cold drinks or light desserts. This level of personalization not only increases campaign effectiveness but also ensures that the chain is always aligned with the consumer's needs and desires, creating a deeper and more personalized connection.

A crucial aspect of applying AI to marketing in fast food chains is the ability for advanced segmentation. Unlike traditional approaches that divide customers into broad demographic groups, AI allows segmentation based on specific behaviors and preferences, delivering individualized campaigns for each group. This results in more relevant messages and offers for each consumer, increasing conversion rates and engagement with the brand. For instance, AI can identify customers who frequently visit during the week but rarely on weekends. Based on this insight, the chain can offer targeted promotions to encourage visits during times when the customer typically does not appear, utilizing more precise and directed marketing.

Another significant benefit of automated marketing with AI is the ability to measure results in real-time. While traditional campaigns required manual and time-consuming analysis to evaluate their effectiveness, AI enables chains to monitor the impact of campaigns as they unfold. Metrics are analyzed instantly, and AI makes automatic adjustments to optimize results. For example, if a lunch campaign is not generating the expected impact in a particular location, the system can adjust the offer or shift focus to more attractive products for that specific audience. This flexibility allows chains to be more reactive and precise, adjusting strategies and campaigns according to customer response and market variables.

Automated marketing with AI also provides integration across the chain's communication channels. With a centralized system, chains can ensure that messages and offers are consistent, whether in mobile apps, social media, or self-service kiosks. Additionally, AI allows these offers to be adapted to specific channels, optimizing how the message is presented to maximize engagement. A customer interacting through the app may receive personalized notifications, while a customer placing an order at a kiosk can see suggestions based on recent choices and peak times.

However, the effective implementation of AI-driven marketing requires intelligent data management. Fast food chains must ensure that customer data collection and storage are conducted ethically and in compliance with privacy regulations, such as GDPR in Europe and similar laws in other regions. Customer trust is essential for the success of any marketing strategy, and transparency about data usage can strengthen this relationship. Additionally, it is important for chains to keep their AI systems updated and properly trained to ensure that analyses are accurate and relevant, avoiding errors that could negatively impact the customer experience.

The use of AI in fast food marketing transforms how campaigns are created and executed. With the ability to personalize each interaction, predict demand, and adjust campaigns in real-time, AI enables a deeper connection between the brand and the customer, increasing loyalty and satisfaction. The intelligence behind these strategies allows chains to operate with greater precision and flexibility, quickly adapting to market changes and making the most of every sales opportunity.

PRACTICAL ACTION

To implement personalization and intelligent marketing with AI, start by mapping the available customer data, such as purchase history, product preferences, and previous interactions. Use this data to develop personalized campaigns and automated interactions that enhance customer engagement and loyalty.

Currently, there are several AI tools on the market that efficiently support personalization and intelligent marketing:

Salesforce Einstein: Integrates AI directly into the CRM, providing personalized insights based on customer behavior, enabling more precise segmentations and automated campaigns that adapt to the customer's lifecycle.

HubSpot CRM with AI: Focused on marketing and sales automation, it is ideal for personalizing interactions and messages based on customer preferences and behavior across various channels, such as email marketing and social media.

Google Marketing Platform: Offers advanced data analysis and campaign automation features, allowing fast food chains to implement personalized actions at scale, adjusting promotions and ads in real time based on customer purchase habits and interests.

Adobe Sensei: A powerful AI platform that provides marketing automation and content personalization, using real-time data to dynamically and effectively adapt promotions and product recommendations.

Marketo Engage: Focused on digital marketing with AI, ideal for chains looking to create highly segmented campaigns and automate lead nurturing flows, increasing customer retention through personalized offers and content.

Amazon Personalize: A solution that uses machine learning to recommend products and offers in real time, adapting to each customer's behavior on online platforms and mobile apps.

Implement these tools to maximize the personalization of marketing campaigns. For example, use Salesforce Einstein to create dynamic segmentations that adjust campaigns as customers interact with the brand, or integrate Google Marketing Platform to automate advertising campaigns that change based on customer location or preferences. Utilize Amazon Personalize to offer product recommendations, adjusting the menu or promotional offers according to the customer's purchase history. Monitor the performance of these tools to constantly optimize marketing strategies, ensuring that interactions remain relevant and targeted to the audience.

Chapter 4 | Inventory Management and Demand Forecasting

Inventory management is one of the most challenging aspects for fast food chains. With perishable ingredients and a constant flow of customers, it is essential for units to maintain the perfect balance between product availability and freshness, avoiding waste and financial losses. Artificial Intelligence (AI) emerges as a transformative tool in this context, bringing precision and efficiency to demand forecasting, automating inventory control, and optimizing the supply chain, ensuring each unit operates sustainably and profitably.

Historically, demand forecasting in fast food chains relied on manual analyses based on past sales patterns and seasonal estimates. However, these traditional approaches are limited and prone to errors, especially when external factors, such as unforeseen events or weather changes, influence consumer behavior. With AI, fast food chains now have the capability to accurately predict demand in each unit, using machine learning algorithms that process vast amounts of data in real-time. These algorithms can identify complex patterns and variables that directly impact consumption, adjusting forecasts as conditions change.

Implementing AI for demand forecasting not only improves the accuracy of estimates but also allows units to make automatic adjustments to their inventory levels and replenishment orders. For example, if AI detects an increase in demand for a particular product on hot days, it can automatically adjust inventory levels to ensure that these items are available in sufficient quantity, preventing stockouts. At the same time, the technology adjusts the replenishment of items that may have lower demand under such circumstances, optimizing storage space and minimizing waste.

This capability for automatic adjustment is essential to ensure that fast food chains maintain optimal inventory levels, regardless of demand fluctuations. Additionally, integrating AI with inventory management systems allows orders to be placed automatically with suppliers, ensuring that products arrive at the units at the right time. This level of automation eliminates the need for frequent manual intervention, enabling unit managers to focus on other operational areas that require attention.

Another critical aspect that AI addresses is product quality monitoring, particularly for fresh and perishable ingredients. AI can track and monitor the shelf life of products in real-time, sending alerts to managers when items are nearing their expiration date or when specific ingredients need restocking. With these alerts, fast food chains can act quickly to use ingredients before they become unusable, reducing food waste and optimizing the use of available resources. The ability to monitor and manage these aspects in an automated manner ensures a more sustainable and cost-effective operation.

In addition to demand forecasting and inventory monitoring, AI is also essential for optimizing the supply chain as a whole. Based on detailed data about delivery routes, transport times, and traffic conditions, AI algorithms automatically adjust routes to ensure that products are delivered efficiently, minimizing delays and optimizing transportation costs. This is especially important for chains operating in multiple locations, where logistics can become complex and costly. By optimizing each step of the supply chain, AI helps ensure that all ingredients arrive fresh and ready to be used, without compromising service quality.

To ensure the successful implementation of AI in inventory management, it is crucial for chains to integrate all their operational systems into a single platform, allowing AI to access real-time data from various areas such as sales, inventory, and logistics. Integration is essential for AI to cross-reference information and make precise adjustments based on interconnected variables. Without this integration, the effectiveness of AI can be limited, compromising forecast accuracy and process automation.

Employee training is also a key factor for successful implementation. While AI automation reduces the need for manual intervention, it is important for employees to be trained to understand how the technology works and how to respond to alerts and recommendations generated by the systems. Managers and unit operators must know how to interpret the data presented by AI and act quickly to implement the proposed solutions, ensuring that operations run smoothly and without interruptions. This ongoing training not only increases the effectiveness of automated systems but also promotes team confidence and engagement in using new technologies.

Using AI for inventory management and demand forecasting also offers substantial financial benefits for fast food chains. By optimizing inventory and reducing waste, chains can cut operational costs and increase their profit margins. Additionally, the ability to quickly adjust inventory levels and product replenishment based on market changes allows chains to maximize sales and adapt to demand peaks, such as during special events or promotions. With AI, fast food chains become more resilient and flexible, prepared to navigate the complexities and volatility of the market.

Inventory management and demand forecasting with AI represent a significant advancement for fast food chains. The ability to automate these processes, continuously adjusting and optimizing based on accurate and real-time data, ensures a more efficient, economical, and sustainable operation. Chains that adopt these technologies not only improve their operational performance but also position themselves competitively in an increasingly demanding and dynamic market. By implementing AI solutions to predict and adjust demand, monitor quality, and optimize logistics, fast food chains can ensure they are prepared to meet customer expectations and grow in a scalable manner.

PRACTICAL ACTION

To optimize inventory management and demand forecasting with AI, start by implementing systems that integrate sales data, seasonal patterns, and external variables such as weather and local events. Use this data to create a predictive model that ensures product availability and minimizes waste, adjusting stock levels in real-time.

Several AI tools currently available offer robust solutions for inventory management and demand forecasting:

IBM Watson Supply Chain: This tool monitors and manages inventory in real-time, using machine learning to predict demand fluctuations and automatically adjust stock levels at each unit.

Microsoft Azure Machine Learning: Offers a flexible platform to create custom predictive models by integrating sales data, order history, and external variables like weather to accurately forecast demand and optimize inventory.

Google Cloud AI: With APIs for data analysis and machine learning, it enables fast food chains to develop customized solutions to forecast demand and automate unit replenishment based on identified trends.

SAP Integrated Business Planning (IBP): Ideal for chains already using SAP systems, this integrated solution predicts demand and manages inventory automatically, providing real-time insights into stock levels and replenishment needs.

Oracle Autonomous Database with AI: Integrates inventory and sales data to create accurate forecasts, using advanced algorithms to adjust stock levels as customer buying patterns and trends shift.

Blue Yonder (formerly JDA Software): Specializing in supply chain solutions, this tool uses machine learning to predict demand and optimize inventory, ensuring that units are efficiently stocked and waste is minimized.

Implement these tools to enhance demand forecasting accuracy and inventory management. For instance, use IBM Watson Supply Chain to continuously monitor units, adjusting stock as sales patterns fluctuate. With Google Cloud AI, integrate external variables like weather and local events to predict demand spikes, ensuring that units are prepared to meet increased customer flow without running out of products. SAP IBP can centralize inventory management, allowing the system to automate replenishment based on real-time data and accurate forecasts, optimizing resources and minimizing waste across the network.

Continuously monitor the performance of these tools and adjust predictive models to ensure that inventory remains optimized, adapting to changing consumer demands and external variables that may impact operations.

Chapter 5 | Automated Logistics and Delivery Optimization

Logistics is the backbone of any fast food chain, ensuring that ingredients and products reach units at the right time and in optimal conditions to maintain quality and efficiency in customer service. In a sector where speed and precision are essential, Artificial Intelligence (AI) is revolutionizing the way chains manage their supply chains and optimize deliveries, transforming complex processes into faster, more economical, and effective operations.

For fast food chains, efficient logistics involves more than simply transporting products from one point to another; it's about ensuring that each unit has the necessary ingredients to operate consistently, regardless of demand fluctuations or unforeseen logistical challenges. In this context, AI is a powerful tool that automates and optimizes logistics operations, using machine learning algorithms to forecast and adjust delivery routes, monitor inventory status in real time, and improve demand forecasting accuracy.

One of the most impactful applications of AI in fast food logistics is route optimization. Previously, routes were defined based on manual analysis and basic forecasts that often failed to account for complex variables such as weather conditions, traffic, or road closures. However, with AI, chains can use algorithms that monitor and analyze these variables in real-time, automatically adjusting routes to ensure products are delivered as efficiently as possible. By avoiding congestion and adapting routes as needed, AI minimizes delivery times and reduces operational costs, ensuring products arrive fresh and within the scheduled timeframe.

In addition to adjusting routes, AI also enables chains to monitor the condition of products during transport. Connected sensors integrated with AI systems can track variables such as temperature and humidity, ensuring that perishable products are transported under ideal conditions to maintain quality. If any parameter falls outside the standard, AI can send real-time alerts so that corrective actions can be taken immediately, preventing product loss and ensuring that each delivery meets the brand's quality standards.

AI's ability to monitor and adjust logistical variables also extends to predictive inventory management. With detailed analysis of historical sales data and continuous monitoring of consumption trends, AI can accurately forecast demand for each unit and adjust stock levels accordingly. For example, during high-demand periods such as holidays or sporting events, AI can anticipate increased consumption of certain products and adjust replenishment orders to ensure units are prepared. Similarly, during periods of low demand, the technology can suggest order reductions to prevent overstocking and waste.

AI integration with the supply chain also allows fast food chains to maintain a centralized, real-time view of their logistical operations. This is particularly important for chains operating in multiple locations and managing supply for numerous units simultaneously. With a centralized and automated system, managers have instant access to data from each unit, enabling them to make quick, informed decisions about how to adjust product distribution as needed. This level of visibility and control is essential for ensuring that operations run smoothly, maintaining consistency and efficiency regardless of the scale of the network.

Automating deliveries with AI also contributes to the sustainability of fast food chains. By optimizing routes and minimizing product waste, chains can significantly reduce carbon emissions associated with transportation and improve the use of natural resources. Additionally, the use of electric vehicles and other sustainable modes of transport, combined with AI optimization, allows chains to become more environmentally conscious, meeting consumers' growing expectations for responsible and sustainable business practices.

Another important aspect of automated logistics with AI is the ability to integrate with suppliers. AI facilitates direct and automated communication with suppliers, ensuring that orders are placed and adjusted according to the actual demand of each unit. Through an automated system, AI generates purchase orders automatically, based on real-time monitored stock levels and demand forecasts. This integration ensures that supply is accurate and agile, reducing reliance on manual interventions and minimizing errors that could compromise the logistics flow.

Despite all these advancements, implementing automated logistics with AI requires careful planning and the integration of robust systems. It is crucial for chains to invest in platforms that can be integrated into all aspects of their operations, ensuring that information flows seamlessly and that AI has access to the real-time data needed to make precise decisions. Additionally, it is essential that the logistics management team is trained to interpret the data and reports generated by AI, responding quickly to any necessary adjustments to optimize the delivery flow.

Automated logistics with AI offers a significant competitive advantage for fast food chains, providing an unprecedented level of efficiency, precision, and sustainability. By automating and optimizing routes, accurately forecasting demand, and integrating the entire logistics management system into a centralized platform, AI ensures that chains operate swiftly and effectively, adapting quickly to market changes while maintaining quality with every delivery. By adopting these technologies, fast food chains not only improve their logistics operations but also position themselves sustainably and resiliently for continuous and competitive growth.

Practical Action

To optimize logistics and automated deliveries with AI, implement systems that integrate traffic data, weather conditions, real-time location, and order volumes, dynamically adjusting routes and delivery methods. Utilizing AI tools allows fast food chains to automate and optimize logistical operations, ensuring fast, efficient, and cost-effective deliveries.

Currently, several AI tools offer robust solutions for delivery automation and optimization:

Onfleet: A delivery management system that uses AI to optimize routes in real-time based on traffic, vehicle locations, and order volumes. Ideal for chains seeking a ready-to-use solution with advanced tracking and reporting features.

Route4Me: This routing tool optimizes deliveries based on factors such as delivery time, distance, and order volume, using machine learning algorithms to adjust routes and maximize efficiency.

DispatchTrack: Focused on delivery planning and management, this solution uses AI to automatically adjust delivery schedules, monitor the fleet in real-time, and ensure that orders reach customers quickly and accurately.

OptimoRoute: A platform that uses AI to create and optimize delivery routes, taking into account traffic and other external factors. The tool allows dynamic route adjustments based on real-time conditions, ideal for operations in busy urban areas.

Google Cloud AI for Logistics: Enables the development of customized solutions for route and logistics optimization, using APIs that integrate traffic, weather, and location data, automatically adjusting deliveries to maximize efficiency.

Paragon Routing & Scheduling: Offers advanced routing and scheduling features, allowing fast food chains to optimize their operations effectively and at scale, using machine learning to adjust routes in real-time.

Bringg: A logistics management platform that integrates and optimizes deliveries, tracks orders in real-time, and ensures a consistent delivery experience for customers, adjusting routes as needed.

Implement these tools to automate and optimize the logistics of fast food chain deliveries. For example, use Onfleet to monitor the fleet in real-time, adjusting routes as traffic and weather conditions change, ensuring that orders arrive quickly and efficiently. With Google Cloud AI for Logistics, create custom solutions that integrate data from multiple sources to dynamically adjust deliveries, maximizing efficiency across all units. Use OptimoRoute to automate delivery routing and adjust paths to avoid congestion, ensuring that deliveries are made as quickly as possible.

Continuously monitor the performance of these tools, adjusting algorithms and routes as needed to ensure the network adapts to changes, maximizing logistical efficiency and providing a consistent and fast experience for customers.

CHAPTER 6 | TEAM AND HUMAN RESOURCES MANAGEMENT

Team and human resource management is one of the fundamental pillars for the success of fast food chains, especially in an industry that relies on high turnover and employees trained to handle fast-paced, efficient operations. With the advancement of Artificial Intelligence (AI), fast food chains now have powerful tools to optimize their team management, from recruitment processes to staff allocation and performance evaluation. AI enables a more strategic and proactive approach, ensuring that operations are supported by an efficient and well-prepared workforce.

One of the biggest challenges fast food chains face is managing fluctuations in demand, which requires frequent scaling and resizing of teams to ensure each unit operates at its maximum capacity without overburdening employees or leaving service gaps. Traditionally, this task was manually executed based on demand estimates, often resulting in staffing errors and either understaffing or overstaffing. With AI, the management of schedules and team allocation becomes far more accurate, as algorithms utilize historical sales data, external variables like weather and local events, and behavior patterns to predict peak and low traffic periods with high precision. With these insights, AI automatically adjusts schedules, ensuring that units have the optimal number of staff for each shift.

Beyond demand forecasting, AI also streamlines the recruitment and selection of new employees. By using algorithms that analyze candidate profiles, work history, and specific skills, AI identifies the most suitable candidates for open positions, matching the required skills to the needs of each unit. This automated resume screening and profile analysis process saves time and resources, allowing managers to focus on interviews and the qualitative evaluation of candidates. AI can also predict employee retention, using historical data and pattern analysis to identify profiles likely to adapt well to the work environment and remain with the team longer, thereby reducing the high turnover common in the sector.

AI's application goes beyond recruitment, extending into the training and continuous development of teams. Automated learning platforms equipped with AI offer personalized training programs that adapt to each employee's skill level and progress. This enables employees to be trained more effectively and in less time, as courses are tailored to meet each individual's specific needs. Additionally, virtual assistants and chatbots integrated into training platforms can answer questions in real-time, providing continuous support throughout the learning process. This personalized approach not only accelerates initial training but also promotes the ongoing development of employee skills, ensuring they are always up-to-date with the best operational and customer service practices.

AI also plays a fundamental role in performance evaluation and monitoring key indicators such as productivity, service quality, and adherence to operational standards. Automated systems monitor performance in real-time, generating detailed reports that help managers identify areas for improvement and recognize standout employees. With predictive analysis, AI can foresee potential issues before they become critical, such as a decline in performance or a risk of turnover. For instance, if an employee consistently shows a drop in performance, AI can suggest corrective actions such as additional training or changes in the work schedule to better align the employee with their responsibilities.

Another important benefit of using AI is promoting team well-being and satisfaction. By monitoring data on work hours, breaks, and workload, AI can detect signs of stress or overload, automatically adjusting schedules or suggesting additional breaks to ensure employee well-being. This level of monitoring and adjustment helps improve job satisfaction and reduce turnover, creating a more balanced and productive environment for everyone. AI also enables employees to provide automated feedback on the work environment, which is analyzed in real-time, offering managers a clear view of the organizational climate and allowing quick adjustments to improve the unit's culture and atmosphere.

Automation with AI also allows the integration of all human resources information and processes into a single, centralized platform. With this integration, fast food chains can access comprehensive data on each employee, from recruitment to ongoing performance, facilitating quick and informed decision-making. This level of visibility is crucial for ensuring that operations run efficiently, even in a dynamic environment with high turnover. Centralizing data also allows networks to adjust their HR policies and practices based on AI-generated insights, ensuring that personnel management is always aligned with operational needs and goals.

However, implementing AI in team and human resource management requires a commitment to training and technological adaptation. It is essential for managers and HR teams to be prepared to use AI tools effectively, interpreting the data and applying recommendations practically. Training sessions and workshops are necessary to ensure that everyone is comfortable using the technology and understands how it can be leveraged to improve the work environment and optimize operations. Moreover, networks must ensure that all HR processes and policies are reviewed and adjusted to align with the new automated approach, guaranteeing that AI is integrated smoothly without friction or adaptation issues.

Transparency and ethics are equally important in implementing AI in human resources. Data collection and employee monitoring should be done ethically and respectfully, always with the clarity that data is being used to enhance the work environment and employee experience, rather than for punishment or excessive control. This helps build trust between the team and the technology, ensuring that the transition to automated systems is viewed as an improvement rather than a threat.

When applied to team and human resource management in fast food chains, AI provides a level of automation and efficiency that would have been unimaginable a few years ago. From recruitment and training to performance evaluation and employee well-being, AI enables fast food chains to operate with a more qualified, satisfied, and productive workforce. By adopting these technologies, chains not only optimize their operations but also create a more attractive and sustainable work environment, ensuring that their teams are always prepared to meet market demands and provide high-quality service.

PRACTICAL ACTION

To implement AI-driven team and human resources management, start by mapping recruitment, training, team allocation, and performance management processes that can be optimized with technology. Use AI tools that support the automation of these tasks, ensuring the fast-food chain maintains an efficient operation and a productive, engaging work environment.

Currently, several AI tools are widely used to optimize team and human resources management:

Workday: Provides comprehensive human capital management (HCM) solutions using AI to analyze employee performance, optimize team allocation, and predict recruitment needs. It is ideal for chains looking to centralize all HR processes in a single platform.

ADP Workforce Now: A tool focused on automating HR processes, including payroll management, performance monitoring, and recruitment support. It uses AI to predict absenteeism patterns and improve overall productivity.

SAP SuccessFactors: Leverages machine learning to enhance recruitment, screening, and onboarding processes, and offers personalized training and automated performance evaluations to ensure continuous employee development.

Oracle HCM Cloud: A robust platform that automates talent management, team engagement, and succession planning. It uses AI to customize training programs and skill assessments, helping identify leaders and develop talent within the network.

Zoho People: A solution tailored for small and medium businesses, automating personnel management processes, including attendance tracking, payroll, and performance management. It uses AI algorithms to predict turnover patterns and suggest corrective actions.

BambooHR: Ideal for networks seeking a lighter and more flexible approach, this tool uses AI to manage the employee lifecycle, from recruitment to performance evaluation and continuous development. It offers insights to improve employee engagement and satisfaction.

Lever: Specializes in recruitment and selection, using AI to automate candidate screening processes, suggesting the best profiles based on the network's specific needs. It is ideal for ensuring faster and more accurate hiring.

Implement these tools to automate and optimize human resources and team management in the fast-food chain. For instance, use Workday or Oracle HCM Cloud to centralize and automate recruitment, monitor employee performance, and personalize training, ensuring teams are continually improved and aligned with the network's objectives. With SAP SuccessFactors, automate the screening and onboarding processes for new employees, adjusting training to meet the specific needs of each unit.

Continuously monitor the impact of these tools and adjust algorithms as necessary to optimize team allocation, predict absenteeism patterns, and enhance employee satisfaction, ensuring an efficient operation and a positive work environment.

CHAPTER 7 | SCALABILITY WITH AI AND AUTOMATED SYSTEMS

In the competitive fast food sector, the ability to efficiently scale operations is essential to maintain competitiveness and support growth. Traditionally, the expansion process involved logistical, operational, and human challenges that limited the speed at which chains could open new units or adapt existing ones for new markets. With Artificial Intelligence (AI) and automation, these obstacles can be minimized or even eliminated, allowing fast food chains to grow sustainably while maintaining quality and consistency across all units.

Scalability with automated systems begins with the integration of technology into all operational aspects of the network. Successful expansion of fast food chains depends on the ability to replicate operations in a standardized and efficient manner across multiple locations, ensuring consistency and quality. By integrating automated systems at every operational level, chains can scale efficiently, maintaining cohesion between units and providing consistent experiences for customers.

AI transforms scalability by centralizing management and operational control. Instead of treating each new unit as an isolated operation, the network can integrate all units into a central system that monitors and adjusts processes in real time. This level of connectivity allows decisions to be based on data collected from all operations within the network, providing a global view of the specific needs and demands of each location. For example, AI can identify regional variations in consumer preferences and automatically adjust menus and promotional offers to accommodate these differences, ensuring each unit aligns with local expectations without compromising the brand identity.

Furthermore, scalability is optimized through AI's ability to adapt quickly to new market realities. When a fast food chain expands into a new area or region, precise adaptation is essential for maintaining competitive performance. AI facilitates this adaptation by analyzing demographic, economic, and cultural data of the area, adjusting marketing campaigns and modifying offers based on the specific preferences of consumers. This flexibility is crucial to avoid the common mistakes made by chains that fail to properly adjust to the demands and characteristics of new markets.

Predictive models are another powerful tool that AI brings to scalability. By analyzing historical and current data, algorithms can predict how a new unit will perform even before it opens. These models take into account a variety of factors, such as population density, consumer behavior, and competition, to suggest adjustments to the operational plan. This allows chains to prepare for specific challenges and adjust their processes before the opening, ensuring the new unit operates efficiently from day one.

To ensure that all units operate efficiently and uniformly, AI can also be used to create standardized operating protocols. Once these protocols are implemented, units can follow the same guidelines, from food preparation to customer service, regardless of location. AI monitors compliance with these protocols in real time, identifying any deviations and automatically suggesting corrective actions. This level of standardization is essential for ensuring a consistent customer experience across all units, regardless of location or time.

Another critical aspect facilitated by AI in scalability is continuous team training. As new units are opened, it is crucial for employees to receive the necessary training to adhere to the brand's operational standards. AI provides automated and adaptive learning platforms that ensure training is quick and efficient, tailoring the content to each employee's needs and pace. Additionally, AI monitors employee progress in real time, providing automatic feedback and suggesting additional modules for those who may need reinforcement in specific areas. This standardized training system ensures that the network maintains service quality across all its units, regardless of location or employee profile.

Logistics automation is another fundamental component of scalability. In a growing network, ensuring that all ingredients and products reach the units on time is a challenge. With AI, chains can optimize their logistical operations in an integrated manner, adjusting routes and distributing supplies efficiently, regardless of the number of units or the distance between them. This ensures that all units receive the necessary inputs promptly, maintaining the quality standard required by the brand.

Throughout the expansion process, it is crucial for chains to maintain continuous performance monitoring. AI enables the central headquarters to monitor all units centrally, checking whether operational goals are being met and if units are following established protocols. If a unit performs below expectations, AI can suggest specific adjustments or proactive interventions, such as localized promotional campaigns or inventory adjustments to meet demand fluctuations. This real-time monitoring is essential to ensure that the network remains competitive and efficient, regardless of the pace of expansion.

The flexibility provided by AI is the key element for sustainable and adaptive scalability. As networks grow, it is essential to have the ability to quickly adjust to new circumstances, whether related to market changes or unforeseen events. AI ensures that operations are agile and responsive, allowing fast food chains to adapt without compromising the quality and consistency of service.

PRACTICAL ACTION

To ensure the scalability of fast food chain operations using automated systems with AI, it is essential to begin by implementing platforms that integrate and automate all processes, from customer service to logistics and inventory management. This approach ensures that expansion into new units is smooth, maintaining efficiency and brand consistency regardless of growth.

Currently, several AI tools are available to assist in automating and scaling fast food chain operations:

UiPath: Specializing in robotic process automation (RPA), it is ideal for automating repetitive tasks on a large scale, such as inventory management, order processing, and logistical coordination. The tool is flexible and can be adapted as the chain grows, ensuring that automated systems keep up with expansion.

Blue Prism: Another RPA solution that helps scale operational processes, enabling the automation of complex workflows like coordinating multiple units and integrating new outlets. It is ideal for networks that need to standardize processes on a large scale.

IBM Watson Automation: Provides an integrated platform for automation and artificial intelligence, helping automate and scale critical operations such as customer service, inventory management, and delivery process optimization. The tool is highly customizable and can be adjusted to meet the specific demands of expanding networks.

Microsoft Azure Automation: Uses AI to automate infrastructure and operations, allowing networks to rapidly scale processes without compromising quality or consistency. With the capacity to integrate and manage different systems, it is ideal for networks seeking sustainable and consistent growth.

Zapier: While not a traditional AI tool, Zapier integrates various applications and systems, enabling task automation across platforms such as CRM, order management systems, and marketing platforms, ensuring that all units remain synchronized during expansion.

ServiceNow Automation: Focused on service automation, this platform enables scaling customer service and support processes, ensuring that new units receive automated and efficient support as the network grows. The tool uses machine learning to continually optimize operations and improve service delivery.

Automation Anywhere: One of the most popular RPA solutions, it is used to automate and scale critical processes such as inventory management and the coordination of multiple units. It offers flexibility to customize workflows and adapt operations as the network expands.

Implement these tools to automate and ensure the scalability of operations across the network. For example, use UiPath to automate tasks like inventory management and data synchronization between units, ensuring that all operations are standardized. With Microsoft Azure Automation, centralize the infrastructure and coordinate the expansion of new units without compromising efficiency or service consistency.

Continuously monitor the impact of these tools to ensure they meet the network's needs as it grows. Adjust automations and system integrations as new units are added, ensuring that scalability occurs smoothly and that all units operate with the same efficiency and quality, regardless of location.

Chapter 8 | Omnichannel Integration: AI in Apps, Websites and Physical Locations

In a market where digital presence is increasingly crucial, fast food chains must ensure that the customer experience is seamless and connected across all interaction channels. Artificial Intelligence (AI) plays a critical role in enabling chains to integrate their digital platforms and physical locations, creating a continuous journey for consumers who seek convenience, speed, and efficiency. This integration goes beyond simply automating processes; it aims to transform each touchpoint into a personalized and coherent extension of the brand.

One of AI's primary functions in omnichannel integration is to create real-time synchronization between different interaction points. When a customer accesses an app, browses the chain's website, or uses a self-service kiosk, all these touchpoints are connected through AI to ensure information flows without interruption. For instance, if a customer places an order through the app, AI ensures that this order is immediately visible in other systems, allowing it to be picked up in-store without the need for repeated steps. This level of synchronization reduces friction and enhances the customer experience, creating a smooth journey where time and convenience are maximized.

AI also enables the integration of data across multiple platforms, which is essential for chains operating in both physical and digital environments. This allows the chain to unify all collected information in a central database, enabling detailed analyses of how consumers interact with the brand across different channels. This data integration allows the chain to not only understand customer behavior but also identify patterns indicating areas for improvement, such as processes that need adjustments to increase efficiency or strategies that could be optimized to engage the audience further. By analyzing these interactions, the chain can create a growth strategy based on concrete insights, focusing on what is most effective for different customer types.

Moreover, AI allows fast food chains to adjust their interfaces and systems according to demand in each channel. When a chain experiences a sudden spike in digital traffic, such as during a special event or promotion, AI automatically adjusts the resources of its digital systems to handle the increased access, ensuring the website and app operate without interruptions. Similarly, if a self-service kiosk is heavily used at a particular location, AI coordinates with other touchpoints to balance the load and ensure that customer service remains quick and effective.

A fundamental aspect of omnichannel integration with AI is the ability to dynamically adapt brand communication. AI adjusts the messages displayed to customers across different channels based on context and the specific situation. For example, if the system detects hot weather in a certain location, it can promote products like ice cream, cold drinks, and other refreshing items, ensuring that the communication is relevant and adapted to the circumstances. This dynamic adjustment increases the likelihood of conversion, as the messages are always contextualized and appropriate for the moment.

Omnichannel integration with AI also facilitates the personalization of offers and promotions, tailoring recommendations based on emerging preferences and the customer's most recent interactions. If a customer accesses the app and searches for special meat options, like Angus beef burgers, AI can identify this preference and, in real time, promote combinations that include these products or related offers. By suggesting these specific options, AI makes the customer experience more relevant and attractive, increasing the chances of conversion without solely relying on historical data.

A significant benefit of omnichannel integration is AI's ability to assist customers in making their choices by using past purchase data to propose specific combinations and adjustments. For example, if AI knows that a customer prefers a burger with extra cheese or usually opts for coffee with sweetener instead of sugar, it can suggest these preferences at the time of purchase, personalizing the experience directly. Similarly, if it identifies that the customer frequently chooses pizza with stuffed crust or likes extra sweet-and-sour sauce, AI can automatically offer these additional options during the order process, making it quicker and more tailored to the customer's preferences. This type of interaction not only facilitates the purchase journey but also makes the customer feel valued and understood by the brand.

Another significant advantage is AI's use in coordinating operations between physical and digital touchpoints, ensuring that resources are allocated optimally. In a fast food chain, it is essential for channels to be synchronized so that campaigns and promotions are effective. For instance, if a promotion is launched on the app and leads to an increase in visits to physical stores, AI can adjust the workflow at the self-service kiosk to meet the additional demand. This ensures that customers arriving due to a digital offer have a smooth, wait-free experience, building trust in the brand and increasing return rates.

Finally, AI enables preventive and automated maintenance of integration systems. All touchpoints in the chain are continuously monitored, ensuring that potential technical issues or system failures are identified before they affect the customer experience. If AI detects that a kiosk is operating slower than usual or that there is an unusual increase in app loading times, it sends automatic alerts and activates remote maintenance processes, ensuring that operations continue without significant interruptions. This proactive monitoring capability reduces downtime and improves operational efficiency across all channels, keeping the chain always ready to serve customers.

In summary, AI enables the creation of a connected ecosystem where all customer interaction channels are integrated, coordinated, and automated to provide a comprehensive and personalized experience. The ability to centralize data, personalize offers, monitor operations, and adjust campaigns in real time ensures that the fast food chain stays ahead, anticipating customer needs and offering agile and relevant solutions. This integrated approach not only enhances customer satisfaction but also allows the chain to operate more efficiently and at scale, maintaining competitiveness in a highly dynamic market.

PRACTICAL ACTION

To effectively implement omnichannel integration with AI, it's essential to unify customer interactions across all touchpoints of the network, whether they are apps, websites, or physical locations. This ensures a consistent and personalized experience, regardless of the channel used by the customer. Implementing tools that utilize AI to collect, analyze, and optimize these interactions in real-time is crucial for personalizing the experience and increasing efficiency.

Currently, various AI tools support omnichannel integration and can be utilized for this purpose:

Salesforce Marketing Cloud: Provides a robust platform for marketing automation and multichannel interaction personalization. Using AI, it enables fast food chains to create personalized campaigns based on customer behavior across mobile apps, websites, and physical points, ensuring consistent communication across all channels.

HubSpot CRM: Integrates customer data collected from different touchpoints, such as apps and social media, and uses AI to personalize interactions in real-time. The tool allows chains to synchronize customer information and adjust marketing campaigns and promotions in an integrated and personalized manner.

Intercom: Focused on multichannel customer support, Intercom uses AI to gather data from interactions in apps, websites, and physical chatbots, ensuring customers receive quick and personalized responses regardless of the service channel. Ideal for chains seeking to centralize customer support and improve the support experience.

Zendesk Sunshine: A solution that uses AI to integrate and manage multichannel interactions, centralizing customer data from mobile apps, websites, and in-person service. The tool allows creating personalized real-time experiences, maintaining service consistency, and adapting messages based on the customer's profile.

Twilio Flex: A flexible communication platform that integrates various interaction channels, such as voice, messaging, and mobile apps, with AI functionalities to personalize and automate service. Ideal for fast food chains looking to manage an integrated customer experience across all touchpoints.

Genesys Cloud: Uses AI to centralize and optimize interactions across multiple channels, such as app service, online chat, and physical chatbots. The platform adjusts messages and interactions based on customer data, ensuring continuous and effective service.

Freshdesk Omnichannel: Focused on customer support and service, it uses AI to integrate customer data and provide a consistent and personalized omnichannel experience. It allows chains to automate service on apps and websites, connecting these interactions with physical service points.

Implement these tools to ensure a consistent and personalized omnichannel experience. For instance, use Salesforce Marketing Cloud to automate and personalize campaigns in apps and websites, adjusting promotions based on customer preferences recorded in previous interactions. With Zendesk Sunshine, centralize customer data and integrate physical touchpoint interactions with digital channels, ensuring customers have a seamless and continuous experience regardless of the touchpoint.

Constantly monitor the performance of these tools to adjust strategies as necessary and ensure the integration between apps, websites, and physical points is running efficiently. Adjust campaigns and messages based on collected data so that interactions are always relevant and personalized, increasing customer satisfaction and loyalty.

CHAPTER 9 | EFFICIENT COMMUNICATION BETWEEN FRANCHISORS AND FRANCHISEES

Communication between franchisors and franchisees is essential for the success and sustainability of fast food chains. Maintaining a clear, efficient, and proactive communication line is crucial to ensure that all units operate according to brand standards, maintaining consistency and quality of service at every touchpoint. Artificial Intelligence (AI) is transforming this dynamic, offering solutions that go beyond simple information exchange. AI enables an integrated communication system that ensures transparency, monitors performance in real-time, and facilitates continuous support, creating a more collaborative and efficient ecosystem.

Historically, communication between franchisors and franchisees relied on manual and often slow systems, involving periodic reports, phone or email conferences, and regular unit visits. This method, aside from being prone to errors and delays, did not allow for real-time information exchange, which limited the responsiveness of both franchisor and franchisee. With AI, this dynamic is transformed through a centralized platform that collects, organizes, and distributes information automatically and efficiently, ensuring that all parties have access to the same, always-updated information.

AI allows franchisors to monitor the performance of all units in real-time, providing precise data on sales, inventory, preparation times, customer feedback, and other critical operational metrics. These data are presented in interactive dashboards, accessible to both franchisors and franchisees, ensuring that everyone is aligned and aware of the network's results and goals. This level of transparency strengthens the relationship between the parties, as it eliminates communication gaps and provides a clear view of operations. As a result, franchisees feel they are part of a well-structured system and can trust the continuous support from the franchisor.

Beyond monitoring operations, AI facilitates the dissemination of best practices and updates quickly and effectively. When the franchisor identifies a practice that is working well in one or more units, they can use AI to instantly share this information with other franchisees, offering detailed instructions and resources for them to implement these practices quickly. This process is automated and standardized, ensuring that all franchisees receive the same guidance, regardless of location. This type of communication enables best practices to be replicated across the network swiftly, improving the overall performance of units.

AI also plays a fundamental role in automating technical and operational support. When a franchisee faces a technical or operational issue, the AI platform can automatically identify the problem based on predefined patterns and real-time data collection. For instance, if a unit shows underperformance due to issues in the ordering system or logistics problems, AI sends automatic alerts to both franchisor and franchisee, indicating the issue and proposing immediate solutions. This kind of automated support significantly reduces response time, minimizes operational impacts, and ensures that franchisees receive proactive and personalized assistance without waiting for human intervention.

Another important aspect of efficient communication between franchisors and franchisees is managing feedback and suggestions. Fast food chains rely on a constant flow of feedback to adapt strategies and improve operations. With AI, franchisees can easily log their observations, suggestions, or concerns directly into the central platform, and AI organizes and analyzes these data to identify patterns and trends critical to the network's success. For example, if multiple franchisees report difficulties implementing a new system or express concerns about the complexity of a process, AI detects these patterns and generates automatic reports for the franchisor. This system allows the network to respond quickly to franchisees' needs, adjusting strategies and procedures to ensure the satisfaction and success of all units.

AI also facilitates the coordination of training and events efficiently and personalized. Instead of relying on manual invitations and decentralized organization, AI automates the process of scheduling training sessions, sending educational materials, and coordinating events, adapting the schedule according to the specific needs of each franchisee. If a unit is struggling to meet its targets, for instance, AI can recommend specific training sessions for that team, offering customized content and flexible hours that fit the unit's routine. This personalized approach strengthens the relationship between the franchisor and franchisee, demonstrating the network's commitment to the continuous development and success of each unit.

Automated communication with AI also simplifies audits and compliance monitoring. In fast food chains, maintaining compliance with operational standards is essential to ensure service quality and uniformity. AI continuously monitors unit processes and sends detailed reports indicating whether each unit is following the established protocols. If any irregularity is detected, AI automatically communicates the issue to the franchisee and suggests corrective measures, while the franchisor also receives an alert to follow up and ensure that the necessary actions are taken. This system reduces the need for frequent physical visits and ensures that units align with brand standards quickly and efficiently.

Another benefit provided by AI is the ability to predict and manage crises, which is crucial for maintaining network stability. With continuous data collection and real-time monitoring, AI can anticipate potential problems before they become critical, such as drops in sales, supply issues, or difficulties implementing new technologies. When these signals are detected, AI alerts both franchisees and the franchisor, recommending immediate actions to prevent these problems from affecting operations. For example, if AI identifies that a unit is experiencing increased customer wait times, it can suggest operational changes or workflow adjustments to correct the problem quickly.

Efficient communication between franchisors and franchisees using AI is more than just an information exchange system; it's an integrated structure that transforms how the network operates. By centralizing data, automating processes, and providing proactive support, AI ensures that franchisees and franchisors work in synergy, maintaining consistency and quality across all units in the network. This level of integration and efficiency strengthens relationships, creates a collaborative environment, and provides a solid foundation for sustainable growth and the brand's continued success.

PRACTICAL ACTION

To implement efficient communication between franchisor and franchisees using AI, it is essential to integrate an automated communication platform that centralizes and simplifies all interactions. AI should be used to ensure that information, updates, and guidelines are distributed quickly, accurately, and uniformly across all units. These platforms should also provide real-time support and enable feedback analysis to continuously improve communication and management practices.

Currently, several AI tools support efficient and centralized communication between franchisor and franchisees:

Slack with AI Bots: Slack is a popular business communication platform that allows the integration of bots and AI assistants. With this setup, it's possible to automate alerts, share guidelines in real time, and manage updates in a centralized manner, ensuring all franchisees receive the same information efficiently.

Microsoft Teams with Power Virtual Agents: Integrating bots into Microsoft Teams using Power Virtual Agents enables the automation of communication and support for franchisees, providing quick responses to common queries and distributing updates automatically. Ideal for networks already using the Microsoft ecosystem.

Trello with Butler (AI Automation): Trello can be used to organize tasks, communications, and processes between franchisor and franchisees. The Butler bot automates repetitive tasks, such as sending notifications about new guidelines or training, ensuring everyone is always up-to-date.

Zoho Connect: A platform that centralizes communication between teams and franchisees, with AI-powered features to automate the distribution of information, schedule meetings, and monitor adherence to the network's guidelines. Ideal for networks seeking an efficient digital collaboration environment.

Zendesk: Used for support and communication, Zendesk leverages AI to organize and respond to franchisee inquiries quickly and efficiently. The platform can centralize FAQs, guidelines, and updates, automating processes and facilitating continuous communication.

Monday.com with AI Automations: This platform allows for the creation of customized dashboards that integrate AI to automate the communication of tasks and guidelines, ensuring franchisees are always aligned with network expectations. Automations enable the automatic sending of notifications and reports.

Intercom: Focused on multichannel communication and support, Intercom uses AI to centralize interactions and manage updates seamlessly between franchisor and franchisees. It allows the automation of alerts and the creation of bots to answer common franchisee questions.

Implement these tools to automate and improve communication between franchisor and franchisees. Use, for instance, Slack with AI Bots or Microsoft Teams with Power Virtual Agents to create automated communication channels that send updates and important information in real time. With Zendesk, centralize queries and support, automating responses and ensuring all franchisees receive guidance quickly and consistently.

Continuously monitor the performance of these tools and adjust communication flows as needed to ensure information reaches all franchisees effectively and uniformly. AI integration should be used to optimize processes and enhance transparency and efficiency in information exchange, ensuring that all units are aligned and operating according to the network's established standards.

Chapter 10 | Training and Retraining Franchisees

Proper training of new franchisees and continuous retraining of current franchisees are fundamental pillars for the success and longevity of any fast food network. The ability to effectively convey best practices, operational guidelines, and brand values is essential to ensure that all units offer a consistent and high-quality experience to customers. Traditionally, training was conducted through in-person sessions, extensive manuals, and frequent visits to units, requiring a significant investment of time and resources. With Artificial Intelligence (AI), this process can be transformed, becoming more dynamic, personalized, and efficient.

The implementation of AI-based automated training systems allows the fast food network to offer an adaptive learning approach that adjusts to the needs and pace of each franchisee. For new franchisees, AI provides a comprehensive onboarding program, covering everything from basic modules on unit operations and the brand's core principles to specific training on customer service, inventory management, and technology usage. AI monitors the franchisee's progress in real time, adjusting content and lesson pace based on performance and comprehension level. This ensures that the franchisee receives a personalized and effective learning experience, quickly acquiring the knowledge necessary to operate the unit efficiently and aligned with the network's standards.

For current franchisees, AI offers continuous retraining programs tailored to the needs and history of each unit. By monitoring operational performance and quality metrics of each franchisee, AI can identify areas that need improvement and provide targeted training for those points. For example, if a unit shows below-expected performance in customer wait times or satisfaction, AI can automatically recommend and schedule a course focused on operational process optimization or customer service techniques. This proactive approach keeps all franchisees updated and in sync with best practices, ensuring efficient and consistent operations across all units.

In addition to tailoring content according to each franchisee's profile and needs, AI also uses interactive simulations to ensure that learning is applied practically and effectively. These simulation modules recreate day-to-day situations faced by franchisees, such as managing high customer traffic, supplier issues, or unexpected operational challenges. Through these simulations, franchisees can practice their skills and make decisions in a controlled environment, receiving immediate feedback from AI on their performance. This type of immersive training helps prepare franchisees for real-life scenarios, increasing their confidence and response capability.

A significant benefit of AI training is the flexibility and accessibility it provides. Franchisees can access content anytime and anywhere, whether through mobile devices, computers, or specific terminals at their units. This flexibility allows franchisees to fit training into their schedules, ensuring they can learn at a pace that is convenient for them without compromising their unit's operations. Moreover, AI allows franchisees to revisit content whenever necessary, ensuring that knowledge is always accessible and up-to-date.

Performance analysis is another crucial advantage that AI brings to training and retraining programs. AI tracks each franchisee's progress throughout the course, identifying strengths and areas that need attention. Based on these analyses, AI adjusts training modules, focusing on content most relevant to each franchisee's development. If a franchisee struggles with a specific module, AI offers additional explanations, support videos, or even supplementary simulations to reinforce learning. This level of personalization is essential to ensure that all franchisees, new or experienced, reach a high level of operational competence and are prepared to handle business demands.

Beyond technical and operational training, AI also enables training in management and leadership skills. These modules are designed to help franchisees become more effective leaders, focusing on skills such as team management, conflict resolution, and strategic decision-making. AI monitors the development of these skills over time, providing detailed feedback and assessments that help franchisees enhance their managerial capabilities. This ongoing development is crucial for franchisees not only to run their units efficiently but also to inspire their teams to uphold the brand's standards and values.

Automated retraining with AI also ensures that franchisees are always up-to-date with the latest innovations and changes implemented by the network. As the brand launches new products, introduces technologies, or adjusts operational processes, AI automatically updates training modules, ensuring all franchisees have access to the latest information and are prepared to implement changes efficiently. This not only facilitates the dissemination of new practices but also ensures that the brand remains innovative and competitive in the market.

Finally, the AI training system facilitates the creation of a collaborative environment among franchisees. AI can organize and manage forums and discussion groups where franchisees share experiences, exchange tips, and discuss common challenges. These AI-moderated spaces ensure that the franchise network remains connected, creating a supportive community and continuous learning environment. This type of interaction, combined with the technical and operational support provided by AI, strengthens the sense of collaboration and unity within the network, fostering joint and consistent growth.

PRACTICAL ACTION

To implement an AI-driven training and retraining system for franchisees, it is essential to use platforms that automate and personalize the learning process, ensuring that content is tailored to the specific needs of each franchisee. AI can be leveraged to create interactive courses, track participant progress, and adjust materials according to each franchisee's knowledge level and performance.

Currently, various AI tools are used to optimize franchisee training and retraining:

Coursera for Business with AI: Offers an enterprise training platform with interactive courses that use AI to adapt content and activities based on the progress and skills demonstrated by franchisees. Ideal for networks that want to offer continuous and up-to-date training.

Docebo: Uses AI to personalize learning and create automated training paths. The platform also allows real-time tracking of franchisee progress, identifying areas that need attention, and providing additional resources to improve understanding and practical application of the content.

TalentLMS with Automated Learning Paths: A flexible platform that uses AI to create and adjust learning paths based on franchisee progress. With automatic quizzes and real-time feedback functionality, the tool ensures franchisees are continually advancing and receiving personalized training.

SAP Litmos: A learning management system (LMS) that uses AI to monitor franchisee progress, personalize courses, and generate detailed performance reports. The platform also enables the creation of interactive modules that engage franchisees and ensure the practical application of learned concepts.

EdApp: Offers a microlearning platform that uses AI to create learning content in small modules, making it easier for franchisees to absorb and retain information. The platform adjusts content based on user performance, providing additional material to reinforce learning.

Cornerstone OnDemand: Utilizes machine learning to personalize training and development programs, monitoring franchisee progress and recommending new courses and modules based on each individual's needs. Ideal for networks seeking continuous and adaptable development.

LearnUpon: An LMS platform that integrates AI to automate the learning process, from course creation to monitoring franchisee progress. With personalization features, the platform adjusts content and provides support to maximize engagement and retention.

Implement these tools to create an automated and efficient training program for franchisees. For instance, use **Docebo** to track participant progress and adjust courses as needed, or **SAP Litmos** to create interactive modules that engage franchisees and ensure the concepts are applied correctly. With **EdApp**, offer microlearning content, facilitating learning in small, easily accessible blocks.

Continuously monitor franchisee progress and performance with automatically generated reports from the platforms, and adjust training to ensure all are aligned with the network's standards and goals. Leverage AI's ability to personalize learning and provide ongoing support, creating a training experience that evolves according to franchisee needs and performance, ensuring effective and consistent development.

Chapter 11 | Franchisee and Franchise Unit Performance Evaluation

Evaluating the performance of franchise units and franchisees is essential to ensure consistency, efficiency, and sustainable growth for a fast food network. However, monitoring and accurately measuring performance continuously can be a significant challenge, especially for networks with a large number of geographically dispersed units. Artificial Intelligence (AI) offers an innovative solution to this challenge by providing an automated, data-driven evaluation system that gives a clear and detailed view of each unit's operation and each franchisee's performance. This approach allows the fast food network to react quickly to issues, recognize and promote best practices, and make informed strategic decisions to sustain its growth.

With AI, performance evaluation is conducted in real time, collecting and analyzing a wide range of operational and behavioral metrics. Among the most critical indicators monitored are daily and monthly sales, service times, inventory management efficiency, customer feedback, and adherence to quality and safety protocols. By integrating these data into a centralized platform, AI provides an accurate and detailed view of each unit's operation, allowing both the franchisor and franchisee to access the most relevant management information immediately. This centralization not only facilitates monitoring but also creates a transparency system that strengthens trust between the parties.

AI is also capable of identifying patterns and anomalies in operational data, signaling when a unit is excelling or, conversely, when it shows issues that require intervention. For example, if a unit starts to show service times above the established standard, AI sends automatic alerts to both the franchisor and franchisee, recommending specific actions to resolve the issue. Similarly, when a unit demonstrates exceptional performance in customer satisfaction or sales growth, AI records these results and shares these best practices with the entire network. This ability to detect and respond to patterns in real time allows the network to maintain efficient and consistent operations across all its units.

In addition to monitoring operational metrics, AI also evaluates the individual performance of franchisees, considering factors such as leadership skills, team engagement, and the implementation of marketing and management strategies. The AI platform can include automated surveys and assessments to gauge franchisees' engagement with the network's initiatives, identifying those who need additional support or who excel and can serve as examples for others. By collecting this data, AI creates a detailed profile of each franchisee, highlighting strengths and areas for development, enabling a more personalized approach with specific training or guidance to enhance their skills.

Another significant benefit of AI-driven performance evaluation is the predictability it offers. By analyzing historical and current data, AI can predict the future performance of each unit, taking into account variables such as seasonality, local economic changes, or regional events. This predictive capability is essential for both the franchisor and the franchisee to anticipate demands, adjust strategies, and ensure the unit is prepared for upcoming challenges and opportunities. For example, if AI identifies that a particular unit tends to experience significant sales increases during a seasonal event, it can suggest that the franchisee prepare additional stock and adjust staff schedules to meet the increased demand, thereby maximizing results.

AI also enables comparative performance evaluation, offering benchmarks for each unit and franchisee to position themselves relative to the network average. This creates a healthy competitive environment where franchisees are encouraged to strive for excellence and implement best practices to meet or exceed established goals. Additionally, this comparative system helps identify units facing difficulties that may need additional support, allowing the network to proactively provide specific solutions, such as training, operational guidance, or process adjustments.

The transparency generated by AI is another fundamental aspect of performance evaluation. With all data centralized and accessible through interactive reports, both the franchisor and franchisee have access to the same information, eliminating doubts and promoting an environment of trust and collaboration. This shared evaluation system allows both parties to work together to improve operations, identifying and implementing best practices collaboratively.

Beyond evaluating individual units, AI also provides a macro view of the network's overall performance. It aggregates and analyzes data from all units, identifying general trends that may impact the brand's growth and sustainability. For instance, if AI detects that several units are facing similar challenges, such as difficulties with service times or inventory inconsistencies, it can suggest global strategies to address these issues, such as launching a new training module or revising operational processes. This global view enables the franchisor to make strategic decisions based on concrete data, ensuring that the network grows cohesively and sustainably.

AI can also reward and recognize franchisees who demonstrate excellence in their operations, encouraging continuous improvement. When a franchisee consistently meets or exceeds sales targets, customer satisfaction, or operational efficiency goals, the AI platform can highlight these achievements and suggest rewards, such as financial incentives or public recognition, fostering a culture of appreciation and motivation. This not only promotes excellence but also sets a standard for other franchisees to follow, strengthening the culture of high performance throughout the network.

PRACTICAL ACTION

To implement an effective system for evaluating the performance of franchise units and franchisees using AI, it is essential to adopt platforms that automatically monitor various performance indicators in real time, such as sales, customer satisfaction, operational compliance, and process efficiency. These platforms should also integrate predictive analytics that allow for the identification of trends and the adjustment of proactive actions to improve performance.

Currently, several AI tools are widely used to optimize the performance evaluation of franchise units and franchisees:

Tableau with AI Analytics: Offers data visualization and analysis with AI capabilities that identify patterns and trends, generating automatic insights into the units' performance. It is ideal for franchisors who want to monitor real-time indicators such as sales, customer flow, and operational efficiency.

Power BI with AI: By integrating machine learning and predictive algorithms, Power BI allows franchisors to create automated reports that analyze the performance of each unit and franchisee, suggesting adjustments to optimize results and identify improvement opportunities.

IBM Cognos Analytics: Uses AI to evaluate performance indicators, generate customized reports, and create automatic alerts for deviations in the operational patterns of franchise units. The tool is highly configurable, allowing precise monitoring of various relevant metrics.

Zoho Analytics: Offers integration with different data sources to monitor the performance of franchise units, with AI capabilities that enable the prediction of patterns and the adjustment of actions to maximize efficiency and customer satisfaction.

SAP SuccessFactors: Used for performance evaluation and monitoring, SAP SuccessFactors integrates AI to generate detailed reports on franchisee performance, adjusting goals, and suggesting specific training to optimize individual performance.

Google Cloud AI for Performance Evaluation: Allows for the creation of custom solutions to monitor key performance indicators (KPIs) and analyze trends based on historical and real-time data. With this tool, franchisors can adjust strategies based on precise predictive analyses.

Workday Adaptive Planning: Provides AI-driven solutions for financial planning and analysis, helping networks monitor profitability and unit performance. The tool generates automated reports that highlight areas of high and low performance, suggesting corrective actions or growth opportunities.

Implement these tools to evaluate and monitor the performance of franchise units in an automated and precise manner. For example, use **Tableau with AI Analytics** or **Power BI with AI** to centralize data and create dashboards that display, in real time, the most important indicators such as sales, service time, and customer satisfaction. With **IBM Cognos Analytics**, configure automatic alerts to quickly identify operational deviations and act proactively to resolve issues before they become critical.

Continuously monitor the data and adjust strategies as needed. Utilize the insights generated by these tools to set specific goals for each unit and franchisee, personalizing action plans to ensure all units align with the network's objectives and operate at their full potential. AI should be used to predict potential challenges and opportunities, enabling the network to adapt its performance management practices quickly and effectively.

Chapter 12 | The Path to ESG Commitment

Fast food chains, traditionally associated with convenience and speed, are currently facing increasing pressure to adapt to sustainable and responsible practices. In a world where consumers increasingly value brands that demonstrate a commitment to environmental, social, and governance (ESG) issues, chains that integrate these principles into their operations gain a competitive advantage and strengthen their market image. Artificial Intelligence (AI) emerges as a crucial tool for these chains to implement sustainable practices efficiently, enabling precise and automated control of various operational aspects that directly impact energy consumption, waste management, and socio-environmental responsibility.

Energy efficiency is one of the central areas where AI can make a significant difference in fast food operations. With systems that monitor and analyze each unit's energy consumption in real time, AI allows chains to identify peak usage periods and automatically adjust equipment settings to minimize waste. For example, AI systems can monitor the operation of ovens, refrigerators, exhaust fans, and other critical equipment, automatically adjusting their power levels or turning them off during low-demand periods. This level of automated control not only reduces operational costs but also helps decrease the chain's carbon footprint, aligning with the sustainability goals that many brands aim to achieve.

Additionally, AI enables fast food chains to optimize their climate control and lighting strategies, which are major energy consumers. By integrating data on climate, occupancy, and peak hours, AI adjusts internal temperature and lighting according to the actual needs of the unit, ensuring comfort for customers and staff without energy waste. For example, on hotter days, AI can predict the increased demand for cooling and gradually adjust the intensity of air conditioning units, avoiding consumption peaks and maintaining efficiency. This approach not only ensures more sustainable operations but also provides significant cost savings, which is essential for chains operating in multiple locations and facing high energy costs.

Waste management is another area where AI can transform fast food operations, promoting socio-environmental responsibility. By monitoring real-time consumption of supplies and waste production, AI identifies patterns and proposes solutions to minimize waste. For instance, the technology can analyze food leftovers and suggest adjustments in preparation processes or stock levels, ensuring that the amount of ingredients used is always aligned with demand. Moreover, AI can monitor the amount of waste generated and propose efficient and cost-effective recycling or composting practices. By integrating these solutions, fast food chains not only reduce the environmental impact of their operations but also align with the demands of consumers who seek brands committed to sustainable practices.

Logistics optimization with AI also plays a crucial role in the sustainability of fast food chains. By managing the supply chain based on predictive data, AI can plan delivery routes that minimize fuel consumption and transportation time, reducing CO_2 emissions associated with logistics. Additionally, AI can adjust the stock of each unit according to the expected demand, avoiding waste and ensuring that products are always fresh and ready for consumption. This not only reduces food waste but also ensures that logistical processes operate at maximum efficiency, positively impacting the chain's environmental footprint.

Another important aspect that AI supports is compliance monitoring with ESG practices. Fast food chains that commit to environmental, social, and governance standards need to ensure that all units strictly follow the established guidelines. AI allows these guidelines to be integrated into operational systems, monitoring whether sustainable practices are being correctly implemented in each unit. For example, technology can evaluate if water and energy consumption levels are within the limits set by the network's sustainability policy and automatically alert when deviations occur. Moreover, it can record efforts made by units to reduce their environmental impact, generating automatic reports that prove compliance with ESG goals. This continuous monitoring ensures that the brand maintains its reputation for responsibility and transparency, which is crucial for gaining the trust of consumers and investors.

The transparency provided by AI also allows fast food chains to clearly and effectively communicate their sustainability efforts and progress. With all data centralized and analyzed by AI, the network can generate detailed reports showing how its operations are adapting to minimize environmental impact and contribute to society. These reports not only strengthen the brand's image with consumers but are also essential for attracting investors and partners seeking companies aligned with ESG principles. By facilitating this transparent communication, AI ensures that the network's efforts are recognized and valued in the market.

AI also enables the creation of engagement and awareness programs for customers and employees, encouraging sustainable behavior both inside and outside the units. Technology can be used to personalize awareness campaigns about recycling, energy savings, and food waste, adjusting messages according to the profile and behavior of each group. For instance, customers using the chain's app may receive incentives, such as discounts, for choosing sustainable packaging options or participating in waste reduction programs. For employees, AI can offer specific training that teaches how to apply sustainable practices in their daily tasks, from waste management to optimizing resource-saving processes.

One of the most promising advancements that AI brings to fast food chains is the ability to innovate in sustainable solutions, such as introducing renewable energy technologies. AI can assess the feasibility of installing systems like solar panels or wind turbines at certain units, based on location and energy consumption patterns. Additionally, by integrating these systems with energy management algorithms, AI can optimize the use of renewable energy, maximizing benefits and further reducing environmental impact. This combination of feasibility analysis and automated management allows chains to become pioneers in sustainable practices, differentiating themselves in the market and gaining the trust of consumers and investors who value socio-environmental responsibility.

Finally, AI transforms the way fast food chains measure and communicate their environmental impact. Technology enables each action to be monitored and evaluated in terms of emissions reduction, resource consumption, and social contribution, generating precise metrics that can be used to adjust practices and set new goals. When shared transparently, these metrics not only demonstrate the network's sustainability progress but also create an environment of accountability, where each unit and each employee understands the role they play in building a more responsible operation.

PRACTICAL ACTION

To implement energy efficiency and socio-environmental responsibility in fast food chains using AI, it is essential to adopt platforms that monitor the consumption of energy, water, and other resources in real time and propose automatic adjustments to reduce waste and enhance sustainability. These platforms should also be capable of analyzing historical data and predicting consumption patterns, helping the chain align its operations with ESG (Environmental, Social, and Governance) principles.

Currently, several AI tools are widely used to monitor and optimize energy efficiency and sustainability:

Siemens Energy Manager Pro: This solution uses AI to monitor energy consumption in real time and analyze patterns, proposing automatic adjustments to reduce waste. It is ideal for chains managing multiple units that need a centralized view of energy use and operational efficiency.

IBM Environmental Intelligence Suite: Offers a comprehensive platform to monitor and manage environmental impacts, such as carbon emissions, water, and energy consumption. It uses AI to predict consumption peaks and optimize resource usage, ensuring that operations align with sustainability goals.

Microsoft Azure IoT Central: Utilizes AI algorithms to monitor energy efficiency and forecast future demands based on historical and real-time data. The platform is flexible and allows integration with sensors that collect information on energy consumption and other environmental metrics, automating adjustments to reduce waste.

Google Cloud Sustainability AI: Part of the Google Cloud Platform, this tool offers AI-integrated solutions to monitor and optimize energy efficiency, as well as assess and reduce carbon emissions. The platform uses predictive analysis to automatically adjust energy consumption in units and minimize environmental impact.

Enel X Energy Management: An energy management solution that uses AI to monitor and optimize electricity usage in real time. It is ideal for chains looking to centralize energy efficiency management and implement sustainable practices on a global scale.

Schneider Electric EcoStruxure: Offers an integrated approach to energy management with AI support, monitoring resources such as energy, water, and gas. The tool identifies opportunities for savings and automation and provides detailed reports for tracking ESG goals.

Johnson Controls OpenBlue: Uses AI to optimize HVAC, lighting, and energy consumption in fast food units, ensuring an efficient and sustainable environment. The tool also generates automated reports on the environmental performance of each unit.

Honeywell Forge Energy Optimization: Focused on energy efficiency solutions, this tool uses AI to monitor, adjust, and optimize energy consumption in real time, reducing waste and ensuring that operations are more sustainable and aligned with ESG targets.

Implementation Strategy

Deploy these tools to ensure efficient and sustainable resource management in the chain's units. For instance, use **Siemens Energy Manager Pro** or **IBM Environmental Intelligence Suite** to monitor energy and water consumption, automatically adjusting usage levels based on demand and external conditions such as climate and occupancy. With **Schneider Electric EcoStruxure**, centralize environmental management and continuously monitor operational impacts, generating automatic reports to measure progress towards sustainability goals.

Monitor environmental performance data and adjust operations based on AI-generated insights. Use these insights to predict consumption peaks and adapt practices efficiently, ensuring that operations remain aligned with ESG objectives. Configure automatic alerts to respond quickly when deviations in consumption patterns are detected, continuously optimizing energy efficiency and the socio-environmental responsibility of the chain.

Chapter 13 | Continuous Evaluation and Monitoring

Continuous evaluation and monitoring are essential pillars for the efficiency and sustainability of fast food chains that aim to quickly adapt to market dynamics and consumer needs. With Artificial Intelligence (AI), the way these networks manage and evaluate their operations is completely transformed. AI provides a continuous and autonomous system that adjusts to the operational environment in real-time, creating a flexible and responsive management model. Instead of relying on periodic evaluations that often fail to reflect the current state of the unit, AI offers a constant and detailed view of all processes, helping ensure that each operation functions optimally.

The use of AI in continuous monitoring allows for the integration of multiple data sources, including but not limited to customer feedback, food quality indicators, and kitchen equipment performance. This integration provides the franchisor with an accurate and dynamic view of how the various aspects of the operation interconnect and influence one another. For instance, if the system detects that a piece of kitchen equipment is operating outside the ideal temperature range, it not only alerts the responsible team for maintenance but also analyzes the potential impact on the quality of prepared foods and the customer experience.

What sets AI-based continuous monitoring apart is its adaptability and learning capacity. As the technology collects more data and interacts with the network, it becomes more precise in its predictions and recommendations. For example, if a unit frequently experiences sales spikes at specific times, AI learns these patterns and adjusts operations accordingly, suggesting automatic changes in staff shifts or food preparation to better meet this demand. This type of adaptive adjustment is essential for fast food chains to optimize their processes quickly and efficiently, responding not only to predicted events but also to emergency situations.

AI-driven continuous monitoring also stands out for its ability to predict and manage risks before they become critical issues. The technology analyzes historical data, comparing it with current performance patterns, and identifies warning signs. For example, if a unit shows an increase in wait times or a higher volume of negative customer feedback, AI evaluates this information collectively and issues alerts that guide the team to take corrective actions. By anticipating these risks and suggesting solutions, AI helps maintain operations within the brand's quality standards and prevents crises that could affect the unit's reputation and financial results.

One of the most unique features of AI-powered continuous monitoring is the real-time evaluation of energy efficiency and resource usage. In addition to monitoring operational performance and customer behavior, AI tracks energy consumption and equipment usage across units. This is critical for chains seeking not only to maximize operational efficiency but also to reduce costs and adopt more sustainable practices. With precise data on energy consumption and equipment efficiency, AI can suggest adjustments, such as optimizing operating times for devices or implementing more efficient technologies. This not only reduces environmental impact but also results in significant savings for the network, increasing profit margins.

The customization of metrics is another key aspect of AI-driven continuous monitoring. Unlike traditional approaches that apply a fixed set of metrics across all units, AI allows each unit to be evaluated according to its specific characteristics. This is particularly relevant for chains operating in various locations and dealing with different customer profiles and market conditions. For example, a unit in a busy metropolitan area may have different service standards and goals than a unit in a rural area. AI adjusts the metrics and benchmarks based on the local context, offering an accurate assessment that considers each unit's particularities. This type of customization ensures that monitoring is relevant and that the AI-suggested actions are specific and applicable to the unit's scenario, enhancing the effectiveness of interventions.

AI-based continuous monitoring also facilitates the integration of new technologies and operational practices smoothly and without disruption. When a network decides to implement new technology, such as an automated ordering system or new kitchen equipment, AI monitors the implementation and the impact of these changes in real-time, assessing whether the new practices are indeed improving efficiency or if further adjustments are needed. This ability to continuously evaluate during and after the implementation of new technologies ensures that the network maximizes the investments made in innovation, quickly adjusting any aspects that are not performing as planned.

Impact analysis is another unique functionality that AI offers in continuous monitoring. When there is a significant change in operations, such as a new marketing policy or the introduction of a new menu item, AI monitors how these changes affect all business aspects, from customer behavior to the operational flow in the kitchens. For example, if a seasonal promotion attracts a higher volume of customers than expected, AI analyzes the positive and negative impacts, such as the increase in sales versus the increase in wait times, and suggests optimizations to ensure the promotion remains beneficial. This type of integrated analysis helps the network make more informed decisions and adjust strategies based on concrete data, ensuring that any change made is supported by solid performance.

AI-powered continuous monitoring is a revolutionary tool for fast food chains, enabling management to be proactive, adaptive, and highly responsive. The ability to integrate multiple data sources, predict risks, adjust operations in real-time, and analyze impacts in detail ensures that networks operate with a level of efficiency that would be impossible to achieve with traditional methods. AI transforms monitoring into a dynamic process that not only reacts to problems but anticipates demands and opportunities, ensuring that fast food chains are always one step ahead in a competitive market.

Practical Action

To implement an effective continuous evaluation and monitoring system using AI, it is essential to adopt platforms that enable real-time tracking of key operational indicators such as sales, energy efficiency, stock levels, and service quality. These platforms must be capable of collecting, processing, and analyzing large volumes of data, providing automatic insights and predictions that allow for proactive adjustments and maintenance of operational quality across all units.

Currently, several AI tools effectively support continuous evaluation and monitoring:

IBM Watson Studio: Offers a comprehensive platform for continuous analysis and monitoring, using machine learning to identify performance patterns and predict operational failures. It is ideal for chains seeking an integrated solution to monitor various aspects such as sales, inventory, and energy efficiency.

Microsoft Azure Monitor: Uses AI to collect and analyze data in real-time, generating automatic insights into unit performance and allowing managers to quickly adjust their operational strategies. The tool is customizable and can monitor a wide range of KPIs (Key Performance Indicators).

Google Cloud Monitoring: Part of the Google Cloud Platform, this tool uses AI algorithms to monitor unit performance and generate automatic reports on operational efficiency, helping identify areas that need immediate improvement.

Splunk: Employs AI to process large volumes of operational data and generate automatic alerts when deviations occur. It is ideal for networks seeking detailed monitoring with real-time visualizations that facilitate decision-making.

Tableau with AI: Tableau integrates AI to offer dynamic, interactive visualizations that display real-time unit performance. With machine learning capabilities, the tool can predict trends and suggest adjustments to optimize operations and improve overall performance.

Oracle Analytics Cloud: Provides a suite of AI solutions to continuously monitor and analyze network operations, offering automated and customizable reports that highlight critical areas and suggest actions to optimize performance.

SAP Predictive Analytics: Uses machine learning to predict events and optimize processes, helping networks continuously monitor unit performance. The tool generates automated insights that enable proactive adjustments and constant monitoring of specific KPIs.

Zoho Analytics: A flexible platform that uses AI to monitor and automatically report on unit performance. It is ideal for networks seeking an integrated and customizable solution for continuous monitoring and trend analysis.

Implementation Strategy:

Implement these tools to ensure constant and automated monitoring of operations. For example, use **Microsoft Azure Monitor** to centralize and analyze data in real-time, quickly identifying any variations that may affect efficiency and service quality. With **Google Cloud Monitoring**, integrate the collection of operational data from all units, creating a centralized view that facilitates management and rapid adaptation to the specific needs of each location.

Continuously monitor data and adjust operations based on automatic insights generated by AI tools. Use these analyses to predict potential challenges and opportunities, allowing networks to adapt quickly and effectively, ensuring consistent and high-quality performance. Configure automatic alerts to act proactively when necessary, keeping operations aligned with established standards and ensuring customer satisfaction across all units in the network.

Chapter 14 | Challenges and Considerations

Implementing Artificial Intelligence (AI) in fast food chains represents a revolution in terms of efficiency, personalization, and innovation. However, while AI offers numerous optimization opportunities, its use also brings several challenges that need to be addressed with careful planning and adaptation. The adoption of advanced technology in such a dynamic and competitive sector requires fast food chains to understand the implications and considerations involved, so they can fully benefit from these resources without compromising service quality, customer experience, or operational structure.

One of the primary challenges to consider is the initial cost and complexity of implementation. Integrating AI systems into fast food chains requires significant investments, both in infrastructure and in staff training. Installing automated kiosks, sensors for inventory monitoring, and connected kitchen equipment are examples of resources that demand not only capital but also meticulous planning to ensure everything works cohesively. For many chains, especially those with more traditional structures or that operate on tighter profit margins, this initial investment may seem prohibitive. The technical complexity of effectively integrating all these systems should also not be underestimated. A lack of technical expertise within the franchise team can complicate the process, requiring external consulting and partnerships with specialized companies to ensure that technology is correctly implemented and systems function in an integrated manner.

Another critical challenge is the management and security of the data collected. With the introduction of AI systems, fast food chains begin to collect a significant amount of information about customers, their preferences, and buying behaviors. While this data is valuable for personalizing service and improving operational efficiency, it also brings risks related to privacy and security. Fast food chains need to be attentive to data protection regulations and ensure that all systems comply with laws like GDPR in Europe or CCPA in the United States. Implementing robust security protocols and encrypting sensitive information are essential measures to prevent breaches and ensure customer trust. Additionally, storing and managing this data requires creating clear policies on how information will be used, with the aim of preserving consumer integrity and privacy.

Employee acceptance and adaptation are other aspects that fast food chains need to address when implementing AI. Introducing automated systems can generate resistance, especially among employees who fear automation may replace their jobs. It is essential for chains to communicate transparently that technology aims not to eliminate jobs but to optimize operations and improve service quality, allowing staff to focus on tasks that truly require a human touch. Investing in continuous training and development is crucial to ensure employees feel prepared and valued in the new work environment. By involving staff in the implementation process and providing them with the necessary tools and knowledge, chains can mitigate resistance and foster a culture of innovation and acceptance of technology.

Customer adaptation to technology must also be considered. Although many consumers are increasingly familiar with using mobile apps and self-service kiosks, there is still a significant portion of the public that prefers human interaction or has difficulty dealing with technological interfaces. It is crucial for fast food chains to implement an AI system that is intuitive and easy to use, providing a smooth transition between traditional service and new automated methods. Offering on-site support, such as assistants to help customers unfamiliar with technology, is a strategy that can facilitate adaptation and ensure a positive customer experience. Additionally, continuously collecting feedback from consumers and adjusting AI systems' interfaces and functionalities based on this feedback is a practice that helps improve customer acceptance and experience over time.

Another important challenge is the maintenance and updating of AI systems. Like any technology, AI systems need regular updates to remain effective and secure. This requires continuous planning and budgeting that accounts for maintenance needs, technical support, and software updates. Chains that cannot manage these aspects effectively may face issues such as operational failures, security vulnerabilities, and loss of efficiency, compromising the return on investment in technology. It is essential for chains to establish partnerships with technology providers that offer continuous support and proactively identify potential failures or areas for improvement.

Another crucial point for fast food chains when implementing AI is the scalability of systems. While AI solutions may be successfully implemented in one or two units, ensuring that the technology works as effectively across a network with hundreds or thousands of units can be a complex challenge. Each unit may have its own particularities, such as location, customer volume, and operational characteristics, meaning the AI solution must be flexible enough to adapt to these variables. Implementing a standardized system that is also adaptable to different scenarios and locations is one of the biggest challenges for chains that wish to effectively expand the use of AI.

Finally, integrating AI with existing systems is a significant technical challenge that chains must overcome. Many fast food chains already operate with point-of-sale (POS) systems, inventory management, and order control systems that were implemented years ago and may not be compatible with the latest AI technologies. Ensuring these systems integrate seamlessly is essential to avoid operational disruptions and maximize AI's benefits. This may involve replacing outdated equipment, adapting software, or even creating custom solutions that connect old and new systems. The complexity of this task should not be underestimated, as failures in integration can lead to data inconsistencies and operational issues that directly impact the customer experience.

Implementing AI in fast food chains offers numerous opportunities but also presents significant challenges that need to be addressed with planning, investment, and a strategic approach. From cost management and employee and customer adaptation to continuous maintenance, system integration, and compliance with privacy regulations, each of these aspects requires specific attention and actions to ensure that the technology brings the expected benefits without compromising operations. For AI to become a transformative and positive element in fast food chains, it is essential that all these considerations are taken into account and that implementation is carried out in a coordinated manner, aligning technology, human resources, and market strategies cohesively.

PRACTICAL ACTION

To overcome the challenges and consider all aspects of AI implementation in fast food chains, it is essential to adopt tools that facilitate the integration, monitoring, and management of AI systems. Selecting the right tools can help reduce initial costs, ensure data security, improve staff and customer adaptation, and efficiently manage system maintenance and updates. These platforms support process automation, compliance monitoring, and system integration, ensuring successful implementation.

Currently, several AI tools are available to support and manage AI implementation in fast food chains:

Microsoft Azure Machine Learning: Provides a flexible platform to create and train custom AI models, allowing fast food chains to tailor solutions to their specific needs, minimizing initial costs, and ensuring scalable and secure implementation.

Google AI Platform: A solution that integrates various AI and machine learning functionalities to develop, manage, and deploy AI models with ease. It is ideal for chains looking to create specific solutions and ensure compliance with data security regulations.

IBM Watson AI Ops: Utilizes AI to monitor and manage the IT infrastructure of networks, identifying potential issues before they impact operations. This tool is essential for system maintenance and updates, ensuring AI systems operate efficiently and continuously.

AWS SageMaker: Part of Amazon Web Services, this platform facilitates the development and deployment of machine learning models, enabling chains to adjust functionalities and ensure seamless integration with existing systems. It also helps manage data security and regulatory compliance.

Splunk AI: Offers a solution for continuous monitoring and analysis of large volumes of operational data, using AI to detect anomalies and generate automatic alerts. It is ideal for chains seeking to monitor performance and ensure the systems adapt quickly as the network grows.

H2O.ai: Uses machine learning to predict patterns and adjust operational processes automatically, helping chains anticipate challenges and optimize AI implementation. The platform is highly customizable and offers support for staff training and integration.

DataRobot: Focused on automating machine learning, DataRobot facilitates the creation and deployment of predictive models, helping chains manage the costs and complexity of AI adoption. The platform also includes features for staff training, aiding adaptation and understanding of new systems.

Oracle AI Platform: Provides a robust infrastructure for developing and scaling AI solutions, integrating process automation and data security. It is ideal for chains that need to ensure operational consistency and compliance as they expand.

Implementation Strategy

Implement these tools to manage and overcome AI implementation challenges effectively. Use **Microsoft Azure Machine Learning** or **Google AI Platform** to create custom AI models that meet the network's specific needs, minimizing costs and ensuring regulatory compliance. With **IBM Watson AI Ops** and **AWS SageMaker**, centralize IT infrastructure monitoring and manage system maintenance to keep operations secure and efficient.

Continuously monitor systems and adjust AI models as needed, using the tools to anticipate potential challenges and implement proactive solutions. With **Splunk AI** and **H2O.ai**, integrate continuous monitoring and data analysis to identify potential failures before they affect operations, ensuring smooth and efficient implementation. Ensure employees are well-trained to operate the new systems, using the tools' training and integration features to maximize adaptation and engagement.

CHAPTER 15 | THE FUTURE OF AI IN FAST FOOD CHAINS

As Artificial Intelligence (AI) advances, the fast food sector is on the brink of an even deeper and more transformative revolution. Emerging trends in AI point to a future where automation and personalization reach unprecedented levels, enabling fast food chains to offer unique experiences while further optimizing operations and reducing costs. The industry is at a crucial moment, where keeping up with technological evolution and adapting to changes is essential to ensure competitiveness and market relevance. The emerging innovations in AI bring immense opportunities but also require strategic vision and preparation to be incorporated effectively and sustainably.

One of the most promising emerging trends is the use of robots in the kitchen, capable of autonomously and precisely preparing food, ensuring standardization and efficiency at scale. These robots are designed not only to replace repetitive tasks but also to improve the quality of preparation by operating with consistent precision, regardless of order volume or peak hours. In a scenario where the demand for fast, high-quality food is increasing, the ability of robots to maintain impeccable consistency in every order offers a significant competitive advantage. Additionally, by automating processes such as frying, sandwich assembly, and dough preparation, chains can redistribute human labor to tasks that require a more personal touch, such as customer service, ensuring that the experience is both technological and human.

Another innovation gaining momentum is automated delivery by drones, which promises to transform how fast food chains manage delivery logistics. This technology is particularly relevant in densely urbanized areas where traffic can delay orders and compromise the customer experience. With the use of drones, fast, precise, and sustainable deliveries are possible as the technology uses air routes, avoiding ground traffic jams. Moreover, drones can be programmed to operate at specific times, maximizing delivery efficiency during high-demand periods. Fast food chains exploring this technology are not only looking to reduce the costs associated with traditional deliveries but also to create a new competitive advantage that positions them as industry leaders in innovation.

As fast food chains incorporate these innovations, it is essential to keep up with the continuous evolution of technology. AI and its applications are not static; they are constantly evolving, and to remain competitive, chains must be prepared to adapt to these changes. This includes not only adopting emerging technologies but also updating and optimizing existing systems, ensuring that the chain's technological infrastructure is always ready to integrate the latest innovations. For instance, as machine learning algorithms improve, it is possible to further enhance customer service personalization and operational efficiency, making the purchase experience smoother and more engaging.

Fast food chains that want to remain competitive in the future must develop a technological roadmap that identifies emerging trends and innovation opportunities that can be explored in the coming years. This strategic planning goes beyond simply adopting new technologies; it involves analyzing how each innovation can be cohesively integrated into the existing operation, enhancing efficiency and maximizing results. The roadmap should include clear goals for testing, adapting, and expanding the use of technologies such as kitchen robots, delivery drones, and advanced personalization algorithms, as well as outlining the steps for system upgrades and continuous employee training to operate in an increasingly automated environment.

In the future, the ability to innovate and adapt quickly will distinguish the market-leading chains from those that fall behind. Emerging AI trends offer not only opportunities to improve unit operations but also create new ways to engage customers and position the brand as a pioneering and relevant entity. Chains that explore these technologies strategically and in a coordinated manner will have the advantage of not only meeting the expectations of modern consumers but also anticipating their needs, creating an agile, sustainable, and continuously evolving business model.

Author's Final Considerations

The fast food sector is undoubtedly one of the most dynamic and challenging industries, where innovation and efficiency go hand in hand to meet the ever-growing expectations of consumers. Artificial Intelligence (AI) emerges as a transformative force in this context, enabling not only the automation of processes but also personalized service, intelligent resource management, and the creation of a scalable and sustainable business model.

Throughout the chapters of this book, we explored in detail how AI can be applied to various critical areas of fast food chains: from customer service to logistics and energy efficiency. The journey of implementing AI requires strategic and detailed planning, considering both the benefits and the challenges associated with the use of advanced technology. Investing in AI means more than just modernizing systems; it is about embracing a future vision where technology and human experience come together to create a more agile, precise, and connected service.

Each chapter was designed not only to explore the possibilities and benefits of AI but also to provide practical actions that enable the direct and effective application of the discussed technologies. In such a competitive and ever-evolving environment like fast food, the ability to adapt and innovate is essential. AI offers this adaptability, but it is crucial for chains to use this technology strategically, focusing on solving real problems and enhancing the customer experience.

Implementing AI in fast food chains is not without its challenges. Technical complexity, initial costs, and the need for integration with existing systems and practices require a careful and structured approach. However, for every challenge, technology also offers solutions. AI tools and platforms are rapidly evolving, and chains that position themselves as innovation leaders will undoubtedly gain a competitive edge in the market.

It is also important to emphasize the social and environmental responsibility that comes with adopting technology. As AI facilitates resource management and energy efficiency, it also paves the way for fast food chains to align their operations with ESG principles, adopting more sustainable and responsible practices. This commitment is essential not only for the future of the business but also to ensure that these chains operate ethically and contribute positively to society and the environment.

Ultimately, the aim of this book was to provide a comprehensive and practical guide on how Artificial Intelligence can revolutionize the fast food sector. Integrating AI into operations, marketing, team and resource management, and energy and logistics efficiency not only enables significant improvements in unit operations but also prepares chains for the future, allowing them to grow sustainably and in alignment with the needs and expectations of modern consumers.

The journey of digital transformation never ends; it is a continuous process of adaptation, learning, and innovation. By adopting AI with a clear and strategic vision, fast food chains are not only enhancing their operations today but also preparing to face future challenges and seize upcoming opportunities. As the author, I hope this book inspires franchise owners and operators to embark on this journey with confidence, leveraging the power of AI to transform their business and positively impact the industry as a whole.

The future belongs to those who dare to innovate and turn ideas into action.

Glossary

AI (Artificial Intelligence): Technology that enables machines to learn and make decisions based on data. AI is applied in various areas of fast food chains, such as customer service automation, demand forecasting, and energy efficiency.

API (Application Programming Interface): A set of protocols and tools that enable different software applications to communicate with each other. APIs are essential for integrating AI systems with existing platforms, such as CRM and ERP systems, allowing for seamless and connected operations.

Automation: The use of technology to perform tasks without human intervention. In the context of AI in fast food, automation may refer to using robots for cooking or systems for processing orders and payments automatically.

Chatbot: A computer program that uses AI to simulate conversations with human users, responding to questions and performing actions automatically. Chatbots are widely used for customer service and order processing in fast food chains.

CRM (Customer Relationship Management): A system that collects and analyzes customer data to improve interactions and loyalty. Integrating AI into CRMs allows for personalized and automated communication and customer service.

ERP (Enterprise Resource Planning): A system that integrates and automates operational processes such as inventory control, finance, and personnel management. AI integrated into ERP systems optimizes these processes based on predictive analyses.

ESG (Environmental, Social, and Governance): Practices that ensure a company's environmental, social, and governance responsibility. AI implementation allows fast food chains to monitor and improve their operations to align with ESG principles.

Integrated Environmental Management Systems: AI solutions that monitor energy consumption and other resources, automatically adjusting usage levels to ensure sustainable operations in line with ESG principles.

KPI (Key Performance Indicator): Metrics used to measure the success of an operation or process. With the help of AI, it is possible to monitor KPIs in real time, adjusting operations to meet performance goals.

Kitchen Robots: Automated devices that use AI to prepare food in a standardized and efficient manner, ensuring consistency and quality in orders. They are part of innovations aimed at optimizing fast food chain operations.

Machine Learning: A branch of AI that uses algorithms to allow systems to learn and improve automatically based on experience, without being explicitly programmed. This technology is used to predict consumption patterns and optimize operational processes.

Marketing Automation: Technology that uses AI to automate and personalize marketing campaigns across various channels, adapting promotions and messages according to customer behavior and preferences.

Microlearning: A teaching method that divides content into small modules or segments, making information easier to absorb. AI-powered microlearning tools are used to train and retrain franchisees, personalizing learning according to specific needs.

NLP (Natural Language Processing): A subfield of AI that enables machines to understand and respond to human language. It is used in chatbots and virtual assistants to enhance customer interaction.

Omnichannel: A strategy that connects all communication channels and sales points of a network, such as apps, websites, and physical locations, to ensure a continuous and personalized customer experience. AI helps integrate and automate these interactions, optimizing the customer journey.

Predictive Analysis: The use of AI to analyze historical data and identify patterns that help predict future events, such as demand peaks or stock shortages. Fast food chains use predictive analysis to better plan their operations and optimize resources.

RPA (Robotic Process Automation): A technology that automates repetitive and operational tasks using robotic software. RPA is widely used in fast food chains for process automation, such as inventory management and customer service.

Route Optimization Systems: Tools that use AI to optimize delivery routes, taking into account factors such as traffic and weather. They are essential for ensuring quick and efficient deliveries, reducing operational costs.

Sentiment Analysis: A technology that uses AI to analyze texts, comments, or customer interactions to identify emotions or opinions, allowing fast food chains to respond proactively and adjust their operations based on the feedback received.

Smart Supply Chain: The use of AI to optimize and automate supply chain processes, such as inventory control and logistics. Fast food chains implement smart supply chains to ensure all products are available efficiently and sustainably.

www.ingramcontent.com/pod-product-compliance
Lightning Source LLC
Chambersburg PA
CBHW050325230526
45471CB00005B/2347